DOT1Q PUBLISHING

Historians on America

Decisions that Made a Difference

George Clack
2/5/2010

Published by dot1q Publishing
Copyright © by dot1q Publishing
Cover Copyright © by dot1q Publishing

ISBN: 978-0-9826266-2-7

The opinions expressed in these essays are those of the authors, not necessarily those of the publisher.

First Printing 2010
Printed in the United States of America

Table of Contents

Introduction

"If you would understand anything, observe its beginning and its development."

—*Aristole*

Historians have used many lenses to analyze how historical change comes about. Thomas Carlyle, the 19th-century British writer, famously defined history as "at bottom the History of the Great Men who have worked there," and he saw heroic individuals as the drivers of change. In the 20th century, the French school of historians known as the Annales (for the journal where they published) reacted against Carlyle and other traditional historians who had presented history as largely a chronicle of wars and political events. In their quest for the roots of historical change, the Annales historians focused on the everyday lives of ordinary people in centuries long past.

Other recent historians have examined technology as a driving force or analyzed the effects of climate, natural resources, and environmental devastation. Under "theories of history," the online encyclopedia Wikipedia currently provides 121 listings.

In this book, we use a different lens—what might be called the tipping-point theory of history, a term borrowed from a recent best-seller in the United States written by the journalist Malcolm Gladwell.

"The *Tipping Point*...comes from the world of epidemiology," writes Gladwell. "It's the name given to that moment in an epidemic when a virus reaches critical mass. It's the boiling point. It's the moment on the graph when the line starts to shoot straight upwards." Gladwell adds, "One of the things I explore in the book is that ideas can be contagious in exactly the same way that a virus is."

Our premise in this book is that by analyzing a few tipping-point events, one can come to a better understanding of not only how the United States became the country it is today but of the values woven into this nation's fabric. From the viewpoint of the present, it is easy to forget that, just 200 years ago, the United States was a fledgling democracy, the recently liberated colony of a world power, with a backwoods economy based on agriculture and exploitation of its natural resources. It's also easy to forget that the institutions, ideas, laws, and values that govern the United States in the present were the creations of individual human beings in a specific set of circumstances.

We asked 11 historians, each an expert in his field, to consider a development that led to the creation of an idea or an institution that is central to America today. Most of the time, our authors find that a heroic individual plays a distinct role: George Washington's decision to retire from the first presidency after two terms guaranteed that the new nation would not have a king. The 1954 Supreme Court decision that led to racial integration of American schools is hard to imagine without Earl Warren as chief justice. The Marshall Plan, which helped bring relief to a devastated Europe after World War II, is certainly well named.

Yet it is also possible to see less personalized and less dramatic transformative events—laws passed by Congress, court decisions, the development of public schools—as examples of the tipping-point theory in action. They occur at times when an accretion of ideas, social movements, economic interests, and other forces have attained a critical mass. When looked at closely, many sudden transformations do not turn out to be sudden.

We do not mean to suggest that historical tipping points occur only in America, of course. By telling these American stories, we hope to provide ways for readers to view history, societies, and institutions in a new light of understanding.

1

The Trial of John Peter Zenger and the Birth of Freedom of the Press

No country values free expression more highly than does the United States, and no case in American history stands as a greater landmark on the road to protection for freedom of the press than the trial of a German immigrant printer named John Peter Zenger. On August 5, 1735, 12 New York jurors, inspired by the eloquence of the best lawyer of the period, Andrew Hamilton, ignored the instructions of the Governor's hand-picked judges and returned a verdict of "not guilty" to the charge that Zenger had published "seditious libels." The Zenger trial is a remarkable story of a divided colony, the beginnings of a free press, and the stubborn independence of American jurors.

❖ ❖ ❖

The Villainous Colonial Governor

The man generally perceived to be the villain of the Zenger affair, William Cosby, arrived in New York on August 7, 1731, to assume his post as governor for New York Province, having been appointed by the Crown. Cosby quickly developed a reputation as "a rogue governor." It is almost impossible to find a positive adjective among the many used by historians to describe the new governor: "spiteful," "greedy," "jealous," "quick-tempered," "dull," "unlettered," and "haughty" are a sample.

Within a year after arriving on American shores, Cosby embroiled himself in a controversy that would eventually lead to Zenger's trial. Cosby picked his first fight with Rip Van Dam, the 71-year-old highly respected senior member of the New York provincial council. Cosby demanded that Van Dam turn over half of the salary he had earned while serving as acting governor of New York during the year between Cosby's appointment and his arrival in the colony. The hard-headed Van Dam agreed—providing that Cosby also would agree to split with him half of the perquisites he earned during the same time period. By Van Dam's calculations, Cosby would actually owe him money—over £4,000.

Governor Cosby responded in August 1732 by filing suit for his share of Van Dam's salary. Knowing that he had no chance of prevailing in his case if the decision were left to a jury, Cosby designated the provincial Supreme Court to sit as a "Court of Exchequer" (without a jury) to hear his suit. Van Dam refused to roll over, and had his lawyers challenge the legality of Cosby's attempt to bypass the colony's established jury system. The decision on the legality of Cosby's meddling with the court system fell to the three members of the Supreme Court he was meddling with, which voted 2 to 1 to uphold Cosby's action.

Despite winning in the Supreme Court, Cosby expressed irritation that the vote for his plan was not unanimous. He wrote a letter to the dissenting judge, Chief Justice Lewis Morris, demanding that he explain his vote. Morris did so, but to Cosby's great displeasure, his explanation appeared not in a private letter to the governor, but in a pamphlet printed by John Peter Zenger. Cosby retaliated by removing Morris as chief justice, and replacing him with a staunch royalist, James DeLancey.

Cosby's firing of Morris intensified the growing opposition to his administration among some of the most powerful people in the colony. Rip Van Dam, Lewis Morris, and an energetic attorney named James Alexander organized what came to be known as the Popular Party, a political organization that would constitute a serious challenge to Cosby's ability to govern.

Cosby attempted to maintain his grip on power by employing Francis Harison—a man called by historians Cosby's "flatterer-in-chief" and "hatchetman"—to be censor and effective editor of the only established New

York newspaper, the New York *Gazette*. Harison defended Cosby both in prose and strained verse, such as this poem that appeared in the *Gazette's* January 7, 1734, issue:

> *Cosby the mild, the happy, good and great,*
>
> *The strongest guard of our little state;*
>
> *Let malcontents in crabbed language write,*
>
> *And the D...h H...s belch, tho' they cannot bite.*
>
> *He unconcerned will let the wretches roar,*
>
> *And govern just, as others did before.*

Besieged by poetry, prose, and the threat of oppression, James Alexander, often described as the "mastermind" of the opposition, decided to take an unprecedented step by founding America's first independent political newspaper. Alexander approached John Peter Zenger who, along with William Bradford, the *Gazette's* printer, was one of only two printers in the colony, with the idea of publishing a weekly newspaper to be called the *New York Weekly Journal*. Zenger, who had made a modest living the past six years printing mainly religious tracts, agreed. In a letter to an old friend, Alexander revealed the *Journal's* mission: "Inclosed is also the first of a newspaper designed to be continued weekly, chiefly to expose him [Cosby] and those ridiculous flatteries with which Mr. Harison loads our other newspaper. ..."

On November 5, 1733, Zenger published the first issue of the *Weekly Journal*. The issue included a detailed account of the victory the previous week of Lewis Morris as Popular Party candidate for assemblyman from Westchester. Morris won the election despite the best efforts of Cosby to rig the election against him by having the sheriff disqualify Quaker voters (expected to be heavily pro-Morris) on the ground that the Quakers only "affirmed" rather than swore the oath required at the time of all voters. The election story, almost certainly written by Alexander, included this description of the sheriff's intervention:

> [T]he sheriff was deaf to all that could be alleged on that [the Quaker] side; and notwithstanding that he was told by both the late Chief Justice and James Alexander, one of His Majesty's Council and counsellor-at-law, and by one William Smith, counsellor-at-law, that such a procedure [disqualifying the Quakers for affirming rather than swearing] was contrary to law and a violent attempt upon the liberties of the people, he still persisted in refusing the said Quakers to vote. ...

No doubt to the surprise and disappointment of Cosby, Morris won the election even without the Quakers' votes. The Journal story recounted how Morris's election was celebrated with "a general fire of guns" from a merchant vessel and "loud acclamations of the people as he walked the streets, conducted to the Black Horse Tavern, where a handsome entertainment was prepared for him."

Subsequent issues of the Journal, in addition to editorializing about other dubious actions of the governor, contained ringing defenses of the right to publish, authored by Alexander, such as this argument offered in the second issue:

> The loss of liberty in general would soon follow the suppression of the liberty of the press; for it is an essential branch of liberty, so perhaps it is the best preservative of the whole. Even a restraint of the press would have a fatal influence. No nation ancient or modern has ever lost the liberty of freely speaking, writing or publishing their sentiments, but forthwith lost their liberty in general and became slaves.

Cosby put up with the Journal's attacks for two months before concluding that it must be shut down. The first effort to silence the Journal occurred in January 1734 when Chief Justice DeLancey asked a grand jury to return indictments based on the law of "seditious libel," a law that allowed criminal punishment of those whose statements impugned the authority and reputation of the government or religion, regardless of the truth of the statements.

The grand jury, however, refused to return the requested indictments. DeLancey tried again when another grand jury met in October. He presented the grand jurors with broadsides and "scandalous" verse from Zenger's *Journal*, but the jurors, claiming that the authorship of the allegedly libelous material could not be determined, again decided not to indict.

Cosby responded to these frustrations by proclaiming a reward of £50 for the discovery of the authors of the libels and by issuing an order that Zenger's newspapers be publicly burned by "the common hangman."

Then, in an effort to get around the grand jury's refusal to indict, Cosby ordered his attorney general, Richard Bradley, to file "an information" before Justice DeLancey and Frederick Philipse, another justice. Based on the information, the justices issued a bench warrant for the arrest of John Peter Zenger. On November 17, 1734, the sheriff arrested Zenger and took him to New York's Old City Jail, where he would stay for the next eight months.

The *Weekly Journal* was not published the next day, November 18. It would be the only issue missed in its publishing history. The next week, with the help of Zenger's wife, Anna, the *Journal* resumed publication with an issue that included this "apology":

> *As you last week were disappointed of my Journal, I think it incumbent on me to publish my apology, which is this. On the Lord's Day, the seventeenth, I was arrested, taken and imprisoned in the common jail of this City by virtue of a warrant from the Governor, the honorable Francis Harison, and others in the Council (of which, God willing, you will have a copy); whereupon I was put under such restraint that I had not the liberty of pen, ink or paper, or to see or speak with people, until my complaint to the honorable Chief Justice at my appearing before him upon my habeas corpus on the Wednesday following. He discountenanced that proceeding, and therefore I have had since that time the liberty of speaking thro' the hole of the door to my wife and servants. By which I doubt not you will think me sufficiently excused for not sending my last week's Journal, and hope for the future, by the liberty of speaking to my servants thro' the hole of the door of*

my prison, to entertain you with my weekly Journal as formerly.

The enormous (in those days) bail of £800 set for Zenger turned into an important tactical advantage for the imprisoned printer. As a result of his stream of "letters" from prison, an outpouring of public sympathy for his cause developed.

The Seditious Libel Trial

James Alexander, who—as the author of the opinions that so offended Cosby—probably should have been in the prisoner's dock instead of Zenger, undertook with fellow lawyer William Smith the task of preparing the printer's defense. Both Alexander and Smith found themselves disbarred, however, in April 1735 by Chief Justice DeLancey after they audaciously objected on the grounds of bias to the two-man court Cosby had hand-picked to try Zenger's case. Alexander recruited 60-year-old Andrew Hamilton of Philadelphia, perhaps the ablest and most eloquent attorney in the colonies, to argue Zenger's case. Hamilton relied heavily on Alexander's behind-the-scenes work, including a detailed brief of the argument that he prepared.

Jury selection began on July 29, 1735, and once again Cosby attempted to influence events by having his henchman, Francis Harison, produce a roll of potential jurors that included 48 nonfreeholders. (Nonfreeholders were persons holding estates at the will or sufferance of the governor, who thus had considerable incentive to produce a verdict that would please him.) The jury roll also included former magistrates and persons in Cosby's employ. This departure from normal procedures was too much even for Cosby's handpicked judges who, sitting behind an ornate bench in their scarlet robes and huge white wigs, rejected the ruse. Twelve jurors were quickly selected.

The trial opened on August 4 on the main floor of New York's City Hall with Attorney General Bradley's reading of the information filed against Zenger. Bradley told jurors that Zenger, "being a seditious person and a frequent printer and publisher of false news and seditious libels," had "wickedly and maliciously" devised to "traduce, scandalize, and vilify" Governor Cosby and his ministers. Bradley said, "Libeling has always been discouraged as a thing that tends to create differences among men, ill blood among the people, and oftentimes great bloodshed between the party libeling and the party libeled."

After a brief statement from defense co-counsel John Chambers, Andrew Hamilton rose to announce that his client—sitting in an enclosed box in the courtroom— would not contest having printed and published the allegedly libelous materials contained in the *Weekly Journal* and that "therefore I shall save Mr. Attorney the trouble of examining his witnesses to that point."

Following Hamilton's surprise announcement, the prosecution's three witnesses (Zenger's journeyman associate and two of his sons), summoned to prove that Zenger had published the offending expression, were

Historians on America

sent home. There followed a prolonged silence. Finally, Bradley spoke: "As Mr. Hamilton has confessed the printing and publishing of these libels, I think the Jury must find a verdict for the king. For supposing they were true, the law says that they are not the less libelous for that. Nay, indeed the law says their being true is an aggravation of the crime." Bradley proceeded to offer a detailed and generally accurate account of the state of law on seditious libel of the time, supporting his conclusion that the fact that libel may be true is no defense.

Andrew Hamilton rose to argue that the law ought not to be interpreted to prohibit "the just complaints of a number of men who suffer under a bad administration." He suggested that the Zenger case was of transcendent importance:

> *From what Mr. Attorney has just now said, to wit, that this prosecution was directed by the Governor and the Council, and from the extraordinary appearance of people of all conditions, which I observe in Court upon this occasion, I have reason to think that those in the administration have by this prosecution something more in view, and that the people believe they have a good deal more at stake, than I apprehended. Therefore, as it is become my duty to be both plain and particular in this cause, I beg leave to bespeak the patience of the Court.*

Hamilton argued that the libel law of England ought not to be the libel law of New York:

> *In England so great a regard and reverence is had to the judges that if any man strikes another in Westmin-*

ster Hall while the judges are sitting, he shall lose his right hand and forfeit his land and goods for so doing. Although the judges here claim all the powers and authorities within this government that a Court of King's Bench has in England, yet I believe Mr. Attorney will scarcely say that such a punishment could be legally inflicted on a man for committing such an offense in the presence of the judges sitting in any court within the Province of New York. The reason is obvious. A quarrel or riot in New York can not possibly be attended with those dangerous consequences that it might in Westminster Hall; nor, I hope, will it be alleged that any misbehavior to a governor in The Plantations will, or ought to be, judged of or punished as a like undutifulness would be to our sovereign. From all of which, I hope Mr. Attorney will not think it proper to apply his law cases, to support the cause of his governor, which have only been judged where the king's safety or honor was concerned. ... Numberless are the instances of this kind that might be given to show that what is good law at one time and in one place is not so at another time and in another place.

His arguments might have been well received by jurors, but Hamilton had almost no law to support his position that the truth should be a defense to the charge of libel. Not surprisingly, Chief Justice DeLancey ruled that Hamilton could not present evidence of the truth of the statements contained in Zenger's *Journal*. "The law is clear that you cannot justify a libel," DeLancey announced. "The jury may find that Zenger printed and published those papers, and leave to the Court to judge whether they are libelous."

In response to DeLancey's ruling, Hamilton revealed the true nature of the defense strategy—jury nullification. With the law on his side of the prosecution, Hamilton hoped to convince the jury that the law ought to be ignored and his client acquitted. The jury's power in this regard, he argued, was unquestioned:

> *[Jurors] have the right beyond all dispute to determine both the law and the fact; and where they do not doubt of the law, they ought to do so. Leaving it to judgment of the court whether the words are libelous or not in effect renders juries useless (to say no worse) in many cases. But this I shall have occasion to speak to by and by.*

Hamilton's lengthy summation to the jury still stands as an eloquent defense not just of a German-born printer, but of a free press:

> *It is natural, it is a privilege, I will go farther, it is a right, which all free men claim, that they are entitled to complain when they are hurt. They have a right publicly to remonstrate against the abuses of power in the strongest terms, to put their neighbors upon their guard against the craft or open violence of men in authority, and to assert with courage the sense they have of the blessings of liberty, the value they put upon it, and their resolution at all hazards to preserve it as one of the greatest blessings heaven can bestow. ...*
>
> *The loss of liberty, to a generous mind, is worse than death. And yet we know that there have been those in*

all ages who for the sake of preferment, or some im-aginary honor, have freely lent a helping hand to op-press, nay to destroy, their country .... This is what every man who values freedom ought to consider. He should act by judgment and not by affection or self-interest; for where those prevail, no ties of either coun-try or kindred are regarded; as upon the other hand, the man who loves his country prefers its liberty to all other considerations, well knowing that without liberty life is a misery. ...

Power may justly be compared to a great river. While kept within its due bounds it is both beautiful and use-ful. But when it overflows its banks, it is then too impe-tuous to be stemmed; it bears down all before it, and brings destruction and desolation wherever it comes. If, then, this is the nature of power, let us at least do our duty, and like wise men who value freedom use our utmost care to support liberty, the only bulwark against lawless power, which in all ages has sacrificed to its wild lust and boundless ambition the blood of the best men that ever lived. ...

I hope to be pardoned, Sir, for my zeal upon this occa-sion. ... While we pay all due obedience to men in au-thority we ought at the same time to be upon our guard against power wherever we apprehend that it may affect ourselves or our fellow subjects. ...

You see that I labor under the weight of many years, and am bowed down with great infirmities of body. Yet, old and weak as I am, I should think it my duty, if required, to go to the utmost part of the land where my services could be of any use in assisting to quench the flame of prosecutions upon informations, set on foot by

*the government to deprive a people of the right of re-
monstrating and complaining, too, of the arbitrary attempts of men in power. ...*

*But to conclude: The question before the Court and
you, Gentlemen of the jury, is not of small or private
concern. It is not the cause of one poor printer, nor of
New York alone, which you are now trying. No! It may
in its consequence affect every free man that lives under a British government on the main[land] of America. It is the best cause. It is the cause of liberty. And I
make no doubt but your upright conduct this day will
not only entitle you to the love and esteem of your fellow citizens, but every man who prefers freedom to a
life of slavery will bless and honor you as men who
have baffled the attempt of tyranny, and by an impartial and uncorrupt verdict have laid a noble foundation
for securing to ourselves, our posterity, and our neighbors, that to which nature and the laws of our country
have given us a right to liberty of both exposing and
opposing arbitrary power (in these parts of the world
at least) by speaking and writing truth.*

Chief Justice DeLancey seemed unsure how to react
to Hamilton's eloquence, founded, essentially, in aspects
of British common law that permitted ordinary people
to have certain privileges and liberties, and theories of
"natural law" propounded during the European enligh-
tenment. Finally, he instructed the jury that its duty under the law was clear. There were no facts for it to decide, and it was not to judge the law. DeLancey all but
ordered the jury to return a verdict of "Guilty":

The great pains Mr. Hamilton has taken to show how little regard juries are to pay to the opinion of judges, and his insisting so much upon the conduct of some judges in trials of this kind, is done no doubt with a design that you should take but very little notice of what I might say upon this occasion. I shall therefore only observe to you that as the facts or words in the information are confessed, the only thing that can come in question before you is whether the words as set forth in the information make a libel. And that is a matter of law, no doubt, and which you may leave to the Court.

The jury withdrew to deliberate. A short time later, it returned. The clerk of the court asked the jury foreman, Thomas Hunt, to state the verdict of the jury. "Not guilty," Hunt answered. There followed "three huzzas" and "shouts of joy" from the crowd of spectators in the courtroom. Chief Justice DeLancey demanded order, even threatening spectators with arrest and imprisonment, but the celebration continued unabated. Defeated, DeLancey "left the courtroom to the jubilant crowd."

Anti-administration supporters hosted a congratulatory dinner for Andrew Hamilton at the Black Horse Tavern. The next day, as Hamilton began his return trip to Philadelphia, a "grand salute of cannon was fired in his honor."

The "Morning Star" of Press Freedom

The Zenger trial established no significant new law and did not, at least for another generation, dramatically re-shape notions of press freedom. Yet, Zenger's acquittal signaled, in unmistakable terms, the colonial public's opposition to prosecutions for published criticism of unpopular officials.

Concern about likely jury nullification discouraged similar prosecutions in the decades following the trial. The Zenger case reinforced the tradition in British and colonial American law that jurors had the power, if not the right, to return a verdict of "Not Guilty"—even when they had no reasonable basis for concluding that the defendant was not guilty of the offense charged. To this day, juries may in effect nullify laws that they believe are either immoral or are being wrongfully applied to the defendant whose fate they are charged with deciding. No trial most famously or forcefully illustrates that key principle of jurisprudence better than the 1735 trial; thus, the trial was a milestone in lending an ethical, or political, dimension to American law.

The effect of the Zenger trial on American ideas and attitudes towards press freedom is harder to measure. Prior to 1735, published arguments for press freedom took a narrow view that suggested protection for printers, but not necessarily for the authors of controversial comments about officials or public institutions. Benjamin Franklin, for example, in his "Apology for Printers" published in 1731 in the *Pennsylvania Gazette*, contended that a printer is primarily the seller of goods, and as such should no more be blamed for selling a publication that contained some dubious and controversial ideas than a seller of pots and pans should be responsible because some of the goods he stocks are less than perfect. A printer, in Franklin's view, served the public by providing information, and should not be seen as endorsing all, or even most, of the views presented in his publication. If someone was to be blamed for dangerous or malicious ideas, the law should focus on the person whose idea is alleged to be troublesome—not the poor printer who is simply trying to make an honorable living.

James Alexander's arguments went much further than those of Franklin. Cosby's chief tormenter matters to the history of our free press not just because of his role in masterminding the 1735 Zenger trial, but also because he became America's first champion of an abstract theory of press freedom that extended beyond protecting printers. In Zenger's paper, Alexander reprinted "Cato's Letters," a series of essays written by two British journalists that presented a reasoned case for a freer press and, especially, for the principle that truth ought to be a complete defense to a charge of libel. Abusers of power, he contended, "sap the foundation of government." To expose such abuses the law should be modified. "Truth," Alexander argued, "ought to govern the whole affair of libels."

Alexander also promoted the cause of a free press in the public mind by editing and printing in 1736 a famous account of the Zenger trial called "A Brief Narrative of the Case of John Peter Zenger." Naturally, Alexander's trial account served to enhance and perpetuate the reputation of both the printer and the Philadelphia lawyer who defended him. The "Brief Narrative" was reprinted 15 times before the end of the 18th century.

However, in spite of Alexander's personal popularity, the trial he made famous neither established the precedent that truth is a defense to seditious libel, nor decisively swung public opinion to a libertarian theory of speech—at least not right away. In the words of free speech scholar Leonard W. Levy, it was a victory for press freedom—like a stagecoach ticket—"good for this day only." With the exception of Zenger's publication, the colonial press remained timid, even when compared to the press of London of the same period. Alexander's essays on press freedom—and he was by no means an absolutist on the question—are among the precious few writings between the period 1735 and the mid-1760s that reflect libertarian thinking on the subject.

In the late 1760s, however, a lively debate about press freedom captured the attention of intellectuals on both sides of the Atlantic. The interest had, as its immediate cause, the policies of the increasingly unpopular King George III. King George's conduct sparked critical comments in the press, together with ever more noisy demands by George's supporters to put a stop to the negative commentary. Looking to history for examples that supported a broader view of the press's role in exposing official abuse, both English and American commentators turned to the famous trial of an earlier generation—the Zenger trial.

Press freedom in America began to blossom. A half-century after the Zenger trial, as members of the First Congress debated the proposed Bill of Rights to the U.S. Constitution and its guarantees of freedom of speech and of the press, the trial would be remembered by one of the Constitution's principal drafters, Gouverneur Morris, the man who wrote the famous words of the Preamble to the Constitution ("We the People of the United States, in order to form a more perfect Union..."). The great-grandson of Lewis, Morris wrote of the Zenger case: "The trial of Zenger in 1735 was the germ of American freedom, the morning star of that liberty which subsequently revolutionized America."

Douglas O. Linder is a professor of law at the University of Missouri-Kansas City, where he teaches courses in constitutional law, free speech, and legal history. Professor Linder has also taught law courses at the University of Indiana-Bloomington and at the University of Iowa. A graduate of Stanford Law School, Professor Linder is the creator of Famous Trials, *a Web site that presents a collection of primary documents, images, essays, and other materials relating to famous trials.*

2

The Constitutional Convention of 1787

On May 15, 1776, the convention meeting in Williamsburg and acting as Virginia's de facto governing body instructed that colony's delegates at the Continental Congress in Philadelphia to introduce a resolution declaring "the United Colonies free and Independent States." That Declaration of Independence from Great Britain, adopted by the Continental Congress soon thereafter on July 4, set the former colonies on an irrevocable course that created the United States of America. But the creation of the United States of America did not occur all at once. Eleven years later, another group of delegates journeyed to Philadelphia to write a constitution for the new nation, a constitution that still defines its law and character.

❖ ❖ ❖

The road from independence to constitutional government was one of the great journeys in the history of democratic government, a road characterized by experiment, by mistakes, but ultimately producing surely the most influential national constitution ever written. Even before the break with Great Britain, the American colonies saw to the nurturing of their future constitutional culture. The lower houses of the colonial assemblies were the most democratic bodies in the English-speaking world, and dialogue with the mother country sharpened the Americans' sense of constitutional issues. For a decade before the outbreak of revolution, disputes over taxes, trials without juries, and other points of contention led to an outpouring of pamphlets, tracts, and resolutions—all making essentially a constitutional case against British policy.

Declaring independence, the founders of American democracy understood, entailed establishing the intellectual basis for self-government. On the same day that the Williamsburg convention spoke for independence, the delegates set to work on a declaration of rights and on a constitution for Virginia. Virginia's 1776 Declaration of Rights was soon emulated in other states and even influenced France's Declaration of the Rights of Man and the Citizen (1789). The early American state constitutions—every state adopted one—varied in their specifics (for example, some created a unicameral legislature, others opted for bicameralism). But they shared a basic commitment to republican principles, principles that then seemed truly revolutionary in most parts of the world—consent of the governed, limited government, inherent rights, and popular control of government.

These early experiments in republican government carried significant flaws. Recalling their experience as North American colonists with British royal power (including colonial governors and courts), drafters of the initial state constitutions reposed excessive trust in legislatures. Checks and balances among branches of government were more theory than reality. Governors were typically elected by (and thus dependent on) the legislative branches, and judicial power was as yet largely embryonic. Another flaw in the original design was that constitutions were drafted by bodies that also served as legislative bodies, thus blurring the line between fundamental law and ordinary law. However, in 1780 Massachusetts took a great step forward in constitutional design when its people elected a convention to write a constitution which, in turn, was voted on in referendum.

The Articles of Confederation

Even more daunting than adopting state constitutions was the framing of a government for the United States. When Great Britain finally concluded a peace treaty in 1783, letting the American colonies go, the nation was composed of 13 state governments. Early nationalist sentiments soon collided with parochial interests, with suspicions of how central power might be used to the disadvantage of individual states. Drafting of a structure to link the states had begun in 1776, but it was 1778 before the Articles of Confederation were adopted and 1781 before all the states had agreed to that document. Distrust of central power was manifest in Article II, which declared, "Each State retains its sovereignty, freedom, and independence, and every power, jurisdiction, and right, which is not by this Confederation expressly delegated to the United States, in Congress assembled."

The Articles created a central government that proved feeble and ineffective. In Congress, each state, regardless of population, had an equal vote. The state legislatures were allowed to decide how delegates to Congress were to be appointed, and a state could recall and replace its representatives at any time for whatever reason it chose. Congress lacked the powers essential to accomplishing national policies. It had no taxing power, having to rely instead on the states' willingness to provide funds—and the states often proved unwilling. The vote of nine of the 13 states was required for Congress to exercise its powers, such as making treaties or borrowing money. Amendments to the Articles required the assent of all the states, giving every state a liberum veto, that is, sufficient veto power to paralyze democratic process. Tiny Rhode Island could thus thwart the will of the other 12 states—as it did in vetoing a proposal to give Congress the power to levy duties on imports.

In particular, commercial rivalries spawned trade discrimination among the states. Landlocked states found themselves at a notable disadvantage, dependent upon states with good seaports. James Madison likened New Jersey, situated between New York and Philadelphia, to "a cask tapped at both ends," and North Carolina, between the deep harbors of Hampton Roads and Charleston, to "a patient bleeding at both arms." The feebleness of the central government was further highlighted by the lack of executive or judicial power to deal with domestic disorder. For example, beginning in 1786, during a period of economic depression, mobs of impoverished farmers in western Massachusetts prevented the courts from functioning and ordering foreclosures. Daniel Shays, a farmer and former revolutionary officer, led a force attempting to seize the arsenal at Springfield but was repulsed. In general, perhaps no flaw in the Articles was as glaring as the inability of the central government to act directly upon individuals, rather than hope for the states to act.

In 1785, Virginia and Maryland appointed commissioners to settle disputes over uses of the Chesapeake Bay and its tributary rivers. These delegates then called for the states to be invited to discuss whether a more "uniform system" of trade regulation might be in their "common interest." Congress responded by calling a meeting at Annapolis in 1786. Only five states attended that meeting, and its members recommended that there should be a constitutional convention in Philadelphia to consider what should be done "to render the constitution of the federal government adequate to the exigencies of the Union. ..." Virginia took the lead in appointing a delegation, and other states followed suit, forcing Congress's hand. Finally, in February 1787, Congress endorsed the calling of a convention. Significantly, however, Congress's resolution said that the convention should assemble "for the sole and express purpose of revising the Articles of Confederation" and reporting to Congress revisions which would become effective only when agreed to in Congress and confirmed by the states.

James Madison and the Virginia Plan

In spite of the innate conservatism of the states, however, once assembled, the convention proved decisive. A remarkable group of 55 men assembled in Philadelphia in May 1787. Their grasp of issues had been honed by wide experience in public life—over half had served in Congress, seven had been state governors, and a number had been involved in writing state constitutions. George Washington, the general from Virginia who had led the war against the British, brought special prestige to the gathering when he agreed to serve as its presiding officer. Other notables included Alexander Hamilton (New York), Benjamin Franklin (Pennsylvania), and James Wilson (Pennsylvania). Perhaps the most conspicuous absence was Thomas Jefferson, who had drafted the Declaration of Independence but who was now serving as the United States' minister to Paris.

It soon became apparent that the most important and respected voice at the convention was that of James Madison, of Virginia. Active in Virginia politics, Madison had acquired a national reputation as a member of the Continental Congress, where he was instrumental in bringing about Virginia's cession of its claim to western territories, creating a national domain. Madison became increasingly convinced that the liberty of Americans depended on the Union's being sufficiently strong to defend them from foreign predators and, at home, to offset the excesses of popular government in the individual states. No one came to Philadelphia better prepared. He had taken the lead in seeing that the nation's best talent was at the convention. Moreover, in the weeks before the meeting, he had read deeply in the experiences of ancient and modern confederacies and had written a memorandum on the "Vices of the Political System of the United States." First to arrive in Philadelphia, Madison persuaded Virginia's delegation to propose a plan which, far from simply revising the Articles, would replace them with a national government of sweeping powers. Deriving its authority from the people, Congress would have the power "to legislate in all cases to which the separate States are incompetent, or in which the harmony of the United States may be interrupted by the exercise of individual Legislation." Further departing from the Articles, the Virginia Plan called for the new Constitution to be ratified, not by the state legislatures, but by conventions elected by the people of the several states.

Resolving themselves into a Committee of the Whole, the delegates debated the merits of the Virginia Plan. Those urging an expansion of national powers, led by Madison and James Wilson, thought it essential to scrap the unworkable system of a central government attempting to effect policy through the states. Instead, they asserted, the national government must operate directly on individuals and, through its executive and judicial branches, be able to enforce its laws and decrees. Principles of individual equality, moreover, called for representation in Congress to be based on population, thus abandoning parity among the states. Madison and his allies were hoping to build upon a sense, widely held among the delegates, that ad hoc or piecemeal reform of the existing system would no longer suffice.

Radical reform was, however, too bold for many delegates from the smaller states. While they might concede the need for enlarging the powers of the central government, including giving it the power to raise its own revenue and to regulate commerce, the smaller states feared domination by the large states. The central question was that of representation. New Jersey's William Paterson insisted that his state could "never confederate on the plan before the committee." With Madison and Wilson continuing to insist on a nationalist plan, it seemed possible that the convention delegates, whatever their agreement on other matters, might founder on the issue of representation.

The Great Compromise and Other Compromises

On June 13, the Virginia Plan, with some revisions, was reported out of the Committee of the Whole. On June 15, Paterson, speaking for the plan's opponents, introduced the New Jersey Plan. Under this plan, each state would have an equal vote in a unicameral Congress. Resolving themselves once again into a Committee of the Whole, the delegates debated the merits of the Virginia and New Jersey Plans. On June 19, the committee voted, seven states to three (with Maryland divided), to stay with the Virginia Plan. The matter remained unresolved, with votes settling into a pattern of six states (Massachusetts, Pennsylvania, Virginia, the Carolinas, and Georgia) against Connecticut, New York, New Jersey, and Delaware, with Maryland divided. In late June, Connecticut's Oliver Ellsworth proposed a compromise—population to be the basis for representation in one house, the states to have equality in the other.

In early July, the convention voted on Connecticut's proposal for state equality in the senate, but the motion failed on an equal division (with Georgia divided). The convention appeared to have arrived at deadlock. Looking for a way out of the predicament, South Carolina's Charles C. Pinckney asked for the appointment of a grand committee. That committee then ratified what has come to be called the Great Compromise— proportional representation in the lower house, states' equality in the upper house. Even while the larger states preferred representation based on population as the basic rule, some of their delegates preferred compromise to risking a walkout by small state delegates. Virginia's George Mason said that he would "rather bury his bones" in Philadelphia than see the convention dissolved without agreement upon a plan of government. On July 16, the convention voted for the compromise, five states in favor, four opposed, one divided (with New York not present).

Notwithstanding grumbling by some delegates from the larger states, the most contentious issue had now been resolved, and the convention could move on to other questions. Election of the executive proved a thorny issue. The Virginia Plan had provided for an executive elected by the legislature; this, however, would create a dependent executive branch—a defect of many of the state constitutions. Few delegates were so bold as to suppose that direct election by the people was a wise move. Ultimately, the convention opted for a device—an awkward one to the modern mind—of having an electoral college choose the president. Each state was entitled, by whatever method it pleased, to select electors equal in number to the number of that state's senators and representatives. The electors would meet in their respective states and vote for the president and vice president. The subsequent rise of political parties, however, has ended the framers' notion that electors would actually deliberate on their choices for national leadership.

On July 24, the convention appointed five members to a Committee of Detail, whose job it was to draft an actual constitution embodying the fundamental principles thus far approved by the whole body. The committee's members seem to have assumed that they were at liberty to make substantive changes of their own. The most important of these was, in place of a general statement of Congress's powers, a clear enumeration of its powers. Leading the list were the power to tax and the power to regulate interstate and foreign commerce—two of the basic reasons that had brought the delegates to Philadelphia in the first place.

Sectional differences surfaced during the convention's latter weeks. Southern states, dependent on the export of agricultural commodities, wanted to forbid Congress's taxing exports, and they wanted to protect slavery and the slave trade. In late August, the convention agreed to a ban on taxes on exports and a prohibition on interference with the slave trade until the year 1808. Slavery was the unwelcome guest at the convention's table. Nowhere does the Constitution use the word "slave" or "slavery." In language intended to compromise competing southern and northern views on representation, the convention decided that, in apportioning representatives, to the number of "free Persons" should be added three-fifths of "all other Persons"—that is, slaves. Some of the delegates thought slavery a blot on the nation's moral conscience, but they concluded, reluctantly, that a stronger stand on slavery would mean rejection of the proposed Constitution in the southern states and thus the prospect of the Union's dissolution. How to resolve the burning issue of slavery was thus postponed, to be settled decades later by civil war and reconstruction.

On September 8, a Committee on Style was appointed to polish the Constitution's language and to arrange its articles. When that committee reported, George Mason, the author of Virginia's 1776 Declaration of Rights, argued that the federal document should also have a bill of rights that would specify and protect the rights of individual citizens. Others argued, however, that nothing in the Constitution would infringe the rights guaranteed in the state constitutions. Mason's proposal was rejected, although it would be revived during the ratification debates.

The convention was moving to its conclusion. On September 17, Benjamin Franklin, at age 81 the convention's patriarch, pleaded with anyone who had some reservations about the meeting's product to "doubt a little of his own infallibility." Looking ahead to the ratification process, the Constitution's proponents wanted a unanimous result. Of the 42 members (of the original 55) still present on September 17, all but three signed the final document. As representatives from each state had concurred in the result, Gouverneur Morris devised the formula "Done in Convention by the Unanimous Consent of the States present" on that date.

How the Federalist Papers Persuaded a Nation

Following the course set out in the Virginia Plan, the Philadelphia convention proposed having the people elect state conventions to pass upon the proposed Constitution. After some hesitation, the expiring Continental Congress forwarded the Constitution to the states for their approval. Once again, as before and during the 1787 convention, Madison took the leading role. Knowing that ratification in Pennsylvania, Massachusetts, and Virginia was critical, Madison helped orchestrate the convening of the state meetings. Several small states, Delaware leading the way, acted quickly, but, as time passed, opponents—known as the anti-Federalists—began to mount their own campaign. Chief among their complaints were the failure to include a bill of rights and the fear that a "consolidated" government would swallow up the states. In carrying Massachusetts, the Federalists acceded to recommendations for amendments which could be added after ratification was complete.

New York seemed especially fertile ground for the anti-Federalists. Madison, Hamilton, and John Jay wrote a series of essays, published in New York newspapers, making the case for ratification. These essays, subsequently collected and published as the famous *Federalist Papers*, stand as the classic exposition of the foundations of constitutional government in the United States. In Virginia, Madison, joined by John Marshall and Ed-

mund Randolph, had to fend off a sharp attack on the
new Constitution draft led by Patrick Henry and George
Mason. The result there was a close one, 89-79. New
York, where Governor George Clinton and his allies bitterly opposed the Constitution, ratified by an even clos-
er vote, 30-27. In eight months, all but two states had
approved the Constitution. Eventually North Carolina
(in 1789) and even Rhode Island (in 1790) ratified. In
the meantime, in September 1788, the Continental Congress resolved that the new Constitution should be put
into effect. In January 1789, the first presidential electors met in the several states, and their unanimous
choice for president was George Washington. In April
1789, Washington was sworn in as the first president of
the United States.

Implicit in the Federalists' campaign for the Constitution was an understanding that a bill of rights—
provisions clarifying the rights of individuals in the new
nation—would be added when the new government got
under way. As a member of the House of Representatives in the first Congress, Madison moved to redeem
that implicit pledge by proposing a list of amendments
to be submitted to the states. Sifting the various proposals which had come out of the ratifying conventions,
Madison produced the amendments which, as ratified,
became the Constitution's first 10 amendments—what
we call the Bill of Rights. Chief among these are protections for free speech and press, freedom of religion,
guarantees of fairness in criminal trials, and the admo-
nition that the listing of specific rights was not to be

read as precluding the existence of other rights retained by the people—a reflection of "higher law" thinking, which, in the 18th century, implied that people had certain "natural" rights.

An Adaptable Document

The Constitution's influence was immediately felt beyond the borders of the United States. The adoption of a written constitution became intrinsically identified with aspirations to self-government. On May 3, 1791, Poland produced Europe's first written constitution, followed soon thereafter by France. Not surprisingly the American experience was often cited in other countries' debates on the drafting of their own constitutions. In Germany, for example, the delegates who met at Frankfurt's Paulskirche in 1848-49 frequently invoked American ideas in shaping their proposed constitution. No one, in France, Germany, or elsewhere, supposed, of course, that one should simply copy the American model. Any constitution, to be viable, must be grounded in a country's own history, culture, and traditions. But the American Constitution, especially as implemented with key interpretations by the courts over more than two centuries, has undoubtedly helped frame debate over fundamental laws in other places.

What contributions did the Philadelphia delegates, and those who have followed after, make to constitutional democracy at home and abroad? Among those contributions are the following:

1. The Constitution, with its explicit reference to its being ordained by "We the People," stands for government based on popular consent.

2. The Constitution declares that it, and laws enacted "in Pursuance thereof," shall be the "supreme Law of the Land." Implemented by judicial review—the courts' power to invalidate laws found to be in conflict with the Constitution—this principle ensures that constitutional guarantees protect minority rights and liberty even against democratically elected majorities.

3. The Constitution's text—and the debates over its drafting—remind us that institution and structure are fundamental to balancing society's need for order with individual liberty. Limited government finds handmaidens in Madisonian concepts such as separation of powers and checks and balances—that is, the apportionment of real power and authority among the executive, the legislative, and judicial branches of government.

4. Partly through practical compromise, the Constitution aims at creating a central government with sufficient energy, while preserving citizens' ability to speak to local issues at the local level. Federalism in its various forms (such as devolution)—that is, the retention of viable state and local governments as well as the structure of a federal government—has proved increasingly attractive as a way of balancing national and local needs in many nations.

Various reasons account for the success of the 1787 convention. Disagreeing on some important issues, the delegates nonetheless largely shared a sense of common purpose. They proved able to rise above parochial interests to serve the greater good. Leadership proved critical. Madison, going into the convention with nationalist goals, was willing to accommodate himself to the convention's result and argue forcefully for the partly national, partly federal arrangement.

Britain's Prime Minister William Gladstone has been quoted as calling the Constitution "the most wonderful work ever struck off at a given time by the brain and purpose of man." That encomium may be a bit rococo for modern tastes, but there is little doubt that the Philadelphia delegates produced one of history's most durable and influential documents. It has proved, as John Marshall, the nation's third chief justice, urged, adaptable to the great crises of a great nation. Scholars sometimes speak of "constitutional moments"—those catalytic events which frame the fundamental contours of a polity. If there are such things as "constitutional moments," then the 1787 convention was surely one of them.

Widely acknowledged as an expert in the fields of constitutional law, comparative constitutionalism, and the Supreme Court, A. E. Dick Howard is a professor of law and public affairs at the University of Virginia. After graduating from law school at the University of Virginia, he was a law clerk to Justice Hugo L. Black of the Supreme Court of the United States. Professor Howard was executive director of the commission that wrote Virginia's current constitution, and he has briefed and argued cases before state and federal courts, including the Supreme Court of the United States. Recent works include Democracy's Dawn *and* Constitution-making in Eastern Europe.

3

Rising by Falling: George Washington and the Concept of a Limited Presidency

In 1797, King George III of England, the British King who had been George Washington's enemy during the U.S. Revolutionary War, appraised his former foe's resignation from the presidency of the United States in March. Referring to this event—and looking back also at Washington's earlier resignation as Command-in-Chief of the Continental Army upon concluding the Revolutionary War, in 1783—George III concluded these two resignations had placed Washington "in a light the most distinguished of any man living." Indeed, the king added magnanimously, that he esteemed Washington "the greatest character of the age."

❖ ❖ ❖

King George doubtless did not have in mind Machiavelli's strategic advice concerning retirement. In his writings, the Italian Renaissance scholar and cynic advised that any general who had won a war for his prince or country should anticipate suspicion. In which case, Machiavelli wrote, the warrior-statesman could save himself in one of two ways: to resign his military powers, thus avoiding envy; or to use those powers to establish himself in supreme office. Resigning, Machiavelli astutely noted, would operate not only to defend against suspicion but also to create a reputation for probity.

Whether George Washington, the first president of the United States, ever read Machiavelli or not, it is clear that he used the power of resignation throughout his career to further his reputation—and his goals for the emerging nation he seemed destined to lead—in ways Machiavelli might have recognized.

Washington began his pattern of resignations from public office when still a youthful commander of the Virginia militia in the early 1750s. His objective at that juncture was to pressure the colonial governor and assembly into providing men and matériel to defend the frontiers against Indian attacks. Yet by the time of his resignation as Commander-in-Chief of the Continental Army in 1783, the more sophisticated Washington had clearly learned to establish concrete political goals that could be advanced by retreating to private life intermittently—just as his goals were advanced by holding public office.

The drama of his public roles combined with the drama of his relinquishments—and his statements at these junctures—magnified the powerful effect his character and example were to have on the entire structure of American government and the future course of American civilization. Notably and crucially, Washington spurned invitations to establish an American kingship in 1782. Following that, when he resigned the military command in 1783, he also made clear that he aimed to continue as a private citizen to found a unified, democratic nation that could secure its "national character"— i.e. a liberal democracy—into the distant future. In his "Circular Address to the Governors of the Thirteen States," of June 14, 1783, Washington phrased his final prayer for his countrymen from the Old Testament verses to be found in Micah 6:8, yet changed those humble words ["What does God ask of man, but to do justly, to love mercy, and to walk humbly with your God?"] so as to embrace the benevolent side of human ambition. Washington prayed:

> *That [God] would most graciously be pleased to dispose us all, to do justice, to love mercy, and to demean ourselves with that Charity, humility and pacific temper of mind, which were the characteristics of the Divine author of our blessed Religion, and without an humble imitation of whose example in these things, we [could] never hope to be a happy nation.*

Washington's phrasing thus converted Micah's humble prayer into a program to shape the liberal character of the United States.

Washington's Ambition

Washington's intellectual ambition sprang from, and was intertwined with, a characteristic personal diffidence noted throughout his career in civil and military office. It has been accepted by historians that the Constitutional Convention of 1787 [see the essay in this volume] was finally able to settle on a constitutional structure containing a strong presidency because of the expectation that Washington would be the first president. Nevertheless, Washington had to be persuaded to attend the convention and then to accept the presidency. Washington during the convention seemed honestly uncertain whether events were unfolding around him—giving credibility to his opinion that "a greater drama is now acting on this theatre than has heretofore been brought on the American stage, or any other in the world"—or whether he himself—no longer a military leader—was still a major player in the drama.

Nonetheless, having been unanimously elected the first president of the United States by the Electoral College in January, 1789, Washington left his Mount Vernon country home on April 16, 1789, and bade farewell to his friends and neighbors in Alexandria, Virginia, with a clear intent to establish an enduring republic. George Washington sought in every way to produce a government for the newly unified states of America that differed from European kingships. In May 1789, he indicated his thinking in a letter to James Madison, one of the primary authors of the new Constitution: "As the first of everything *in our situation* will serve to establish a precedent, it is devoutly to be wished on my part, that these precedents may be fixed on true principles."

Thus, the first inaugural address of his presidency focused almost exclusively upon the responsibilities—not the powers of the officers of the new U.S. government. However, Washington realized that democracy, if wary of autocracy, could scarcely tolerate anarchy. Corresponding with the growth of political parties and increasing dissension in the new republic as the years passed, Washington devoted much thought to the survival of the nation as a successful political entity, including his much remarked 1794 "State of the Union" address in which he condemned "self-created democratic societies" that had been implicated in the Whisky Rebellion. This minor revolt of 500 farmers in Pennsylvania against a federal liquor tax had been one of the first tests for the new national government. When Washington ordered troops into the area, the opposition collapsed without a fight. Still, these "self-created democratic societies" seemed to him at the time to contain the potential for something like the terror spawned by the French Revolution. Besides protesting a federal tax on distilled spirits with populist, rejectionist political rhetoric, the farmers had seemed to be influenced by the French ambassador, Edmond Genet, who had directly challenged Washington's authority by threatening an appeal to the people to override Washington's "Proclamation of Neutrality" in the looming war between England and France.

In addition, Washington realized a successful democracy would require a competent and forceful executive. Washington's attempt to balance humility with firmness was not always easy to achieve. Organizing the new government with exquisite attention to the symbolic significance of every word and deed for subsequent practice required fortitude and an iron will. The U.S. Constitution mandates that the executive branch will seek the "advice and consent" of the Senate to treaties with foreign powers. Thus, Washington as president once determined to "advise and consult" with the Senate on a treaty matter involving negotiations with Indian tribes. Accompanied by his secretary of war, Henry Knox, the president presented himself before the Senate while the clerk read out the main points that concerned Washington—thus seeking the point-by-point constitutional "advice and consent." Following this dramatic entrance, Washington was ushered out of the chamber and cooled his heels *outside* while what was later to become known as the "world's greatest deliberative body" debated how to proceed. Realizing he'd made a mistake that could limit the power and authority of future presidents, the president turned on his heels and left the building—never to return personally before the Senate for such purposes. By doing so, Washington took a firm step towards creating a presidency that is strong, dignified, and autonomous within a system of checks and balances, while responsive to Congress through intermediaries. This simple act helped define the future balance of power between the executive and legislative branches of the U.S. government.

Moderation and Magnanimity

While aware that the success of the new federal government depended on a strong presidency, Washington, as noted, took steps to make sure future presidents would not become autocrats. He did this by attempting to define the character of the new federal government as much as the office of the presidency—or, as he put it, "to express my idea of a flourishing state with precision; and to distinguish between happiness and splendor." That distinction had already constituted the animating theme of the 1783 "Circular Address"—democratic self-government understood as requiring a spirit of moderation to survive and thrive. To moderation, he had added a spirit of "magnanimity," a spirit that enables democratic government to seek restraint and compromise, and to avoid demanding total power. (Washington later praised and encouraged the same "magnanimity" in his 1796 Farewell Address.)

Parsing the history of the Declaration of Independence, Washington declared in the 1789 draft inaugural address:

> *I rejoice in a belief that intellectual light will spring up in the dark corners of the earth; that freedom of en-*

quiry will produce liberality of conduct; that mankind will reverse the absurd position that the many were, made for the few; and that they will not continue slaves in one part of the globe, when they can become freemen in another.

He continued in the 1789 draft inaugural address to set forth his intentions for the presidency. Washington desired, he explained, to assume the presidency in the company of fellow citizens, entering a path that would yet prove "intricate and thorny," but which would "grow plain and smooth as we go." It would grow so, he held, because of adhering to that "eternal line that separates right from wrong." When the time came, therefore, for his retirement from the presidency in 1796, which established the precedent of the two-term (eight year) presidency, all the elements of a moral view of the office and the entire federal structure had been established to give his retirement the decisive and dramatic significance that it has had ever since in the United States.

Washington's administration of the presidency under the new federal Constitution was not untroubled. During the eight years he held office, the founding of a new nation itself was consummated, yet, during that same time, Americans witnessed the birth of what ultimately became political parties. Washington's unanimous election to the presidency by the representatives of a grateful nation was never to be repeated, as other statesmen of the era discovered room to contest his "administration" of the government within the protective confines of the Constitution. As the new democracy splintered into what he called "factions," Washington himself became the tacit head of the Federalist Party, direct heir to the Federalists, the advocates of the new Constitution who had prevailed in the struggle over whether the states would ratify it.

The opposition party, the Democratic-Republican Party, was headed by James Madison and Thomas Jefferson. For all but the first two years of Washington's time in office as president, growing party discord figured as the most significant and most pressing political development. The country witnessed the emergence of party presses and party organizations. Whereas nowadays it is assumed that the executive branch of government consists of the president's supporters, in those days, the executive branch itself was divided. Alexander Hamilton, secretary of the treasury, managed the Federalists, while Thomas Jefferson spearheaded the opposition Republicans, even while he was secretary of state in Washington's cabinet. Madison, whose 1791-92 essays in the *National Gazette* laid out the Republican platform, had previously been the principal Federalist spokesman in Congress. To all appearances, therefore, the cemented union for which Washington had so long labored was being fractured in a contest over the spoils of victory. While maintaining the principle of energetic debate, Washington sought to contain the damage of uncontrolled division, praying that "the cup which has been presented may not be snatched from our lips by a discordance of action." The fact that this discord of the early Republic was ultimately contained "within the walls of the Constitution" is perhaps the single greatest achievement of the founding, and of Washington's presidency.

A Definitive Retirement

With a presidential election and the prospect of a third term of office looming before him, Washington determined to retire in 1796. While making this decision, he planned how his retirement in this instance could become a permanent advantage to the new American state. On May 10, 1796, he asked Alexander Hamilton to help prepare a valedictory address. Washington sent to Hamilton a draft, parts of which had been authored by James Madison four years earlier (prematurely as it turned out). After four months of correspondence, Washington's objective had been achieved, and he published the "Farewell" on Monday, September 17, 1796—Constitution Day—in *Claypoole's American Daily Advertiser.*

Washington confidently speaks of "the happy reward of our mutual cares, labors, and dangers" in his "Farewell Address," making it clear that he was leaving the office of the presidency with no less ease of spirit than he mustered when he resigned his military commission in 1783. On the earlier occasion Washington declared that he resigned "with satisfaction the appointment [he] accepted with diffidence." Washington presented his retirement from the presidency in the following light:

1. The period for a new election to the presidency was drawing near, and Washington chose to "further public deliberation" by declaring his unavailability.

2. His was the path of "duty" as well as "inclination."

3. Previously, duty had always overridden inclination, as in the case when the critical posture of "our affairs with foreign nations" prevented a retirement in 1792.

4. By 1796 the people's "external and internal" concerns were compatible with releasing him.

5. He had explained in his first inaugural address the end that he had in view and retired believing that he had succeeded, but attributed success to "the people."

6. He was grateful for the success of "your" efforts and wished that "your union" and "brotherly affection" might be perpetual; so that the free constitution which was the work of "your hands" might be sacredly maintained; and so that "the happiness of the people of these States, under the auspices of liberty," might be made complete by "so prudent a use of this blessing."

Finally, desiring "the permanency" of "your happiness as a people," he offered disinterested advice similar to that he urged when he disbanded the army.

On that occasion, Washington, drafting his 1783 "Circular Address," was responding to the urgings of several of his colleagues to leave his countrymen a political testament to guide their future considerations. Washington acknowledged these urgings in a letter to Robert Morris on June 3, 1783, by stating that he would "with greatest freedom give my sentiments to the States on several political subjects." He followed the same model in 1796, upon leaving the presidency, without need of urging.

Washington's retirement from the presidency in 1796 after two four-year terms in office was important because it cemented the concept of a limited presidency. Washington could have used his military stature and his enormous popularity to become an autocrat; yet, he refused to do so. His modesty certainly appealed to the public. The spontaneous and universal acclaim that welcomed him home from the Revolutionary War in 1783 was duplicated on this occasion.

This time, however, he had completed a much more trying task, the increasingly bitter party strife having made even him an open target. Not only had the country been solidified and its finances put in order, but also ominous threats of foreign war that loomed over his last five years in office had greatly declined even while the country had been strengthened. Washington also took satisfaction that resignation removed him from that unfamiliar position of being held up to public scorn and ridicule by "infamous scribblers," a source of grief and irritation to every president since Washington as well.

The Rise of the People

In evaluating the strength of Washington's character in the presidency, and his contribution to the foundation of a democratic republic, one might mention an incident from his earlier years. He had ended his military career as the revolutionary commander with a poignant fare-well to the officers who had served faithfully under him. Woodrow Wilson noted that, in the final years of the Revolutionary War and "the absence of any real government, Washington proved almost the only prop of authority and law." How this arose from Washington's character was displayed fully in Fraunces Tavern, November 23, 1783. The British had departed New York, and the general bade farewell to his men. At that emotional moment, at a loss for words, according to contemporary accounts, Washington raised his glass: "With heart full of love and gratitude, I now take my leave of you." He extended his hand, to shake the hands of his officers filing past. Henry Knox stood nearest and, when the moment came to shake hands and pass, Washington impulsively embraced and kissed that faithful general.

Then, in perfect silence, he so embraced each of his officers as they filed by, and then they parted. This dramatic end to eight years of bloody travail demonstrates Washington's instinctive wish to build concord out of conflict, and his ability to recognize the merit and value of others, as well as his own.

When Washington declared, upon retiring from the presidency decades later, that "'Tis substantially true, that virtue or morality is a necessary spring of popular government," he stated in words what his earlier actions symbolized: that the success of the democratic enterprise depends on a certain willingness to give others their due and to relinquish some claims of the ego and of power. The very first condition for the preservation

50

of a democratic republic, Washington believed, is the foundation within the individual of prudent reason. Speaking of the people as a whole, Washington ultimately called this quality "enlightened opinion" and "national morality."

By commending morality and reason to the American people as he left office, Washington hoped that the power of his example had made them capable of following duty over inclination. By limiting his own behavior and prerogatives in office and by enduring conflict without resorting to tyranny, Washington made it clear that he wished his legacy to be a true democracy, and not a reversion to traditional autocracy. His refusal to seek a third presidential term cemented that. Washington's "falling" in 1796 was his people's rising. Continuing respect for the two-term presidential precedent in the United States (now enforced by constitutional amendment) represents continuing affirmation of the people's authority.

W. B. Allen is a professor of political science at Michigan State University, specializing in political philosophy, American government, and jurisprudence. Currently on sabbatical leave, he is a visiting fellow in the James Madison Program, Department of Politics, Princeton University, translating Montesquieu's Spirit of the Laws. *His publications include* George Washington: A Collection, *and* Habits of Mind: Fostering Access and Excellence in Higher Education *(with Carol M. Allen).*

4

Victory of the Common School Movement: A Turning Point in American Educational History

Americans today count on their public schools to be free of expense, open to all, and devoid of religious sectarianism. Although families are permitted to enroll their children in private schools at their own expense in the United States, the percentage of private school students has been stable at about 10-12 percent for half a century. The great majority of students attend public schools, from the first to the twelfth year of schooling, the fulfillment of a crucial policy decision made in each individual state in the northern part of the country in the 1840s, and in the southern states in the late nineteenth century. It was called "the common school movement."

❖ ❖ ❖

Free schools open to all children did not exist in colonial America. Yet, something like modern American public schools developed in the 1840s, when a majority of voters in the northern regions of the United States decided that it would be wise to create state-mandated and locally controlled free schools. Once this model of schooling prevailed, the stage was set for the creation of an inclusive free-school system in the United States.

In the British colonies of the 17th and 18th centuries, schooling was not compulsory, not free of charge, not secular, not open to all, and not even central to most children's education. Decisions about the provision of schools were made town-by-town. Girls were often excluded, or allowed to attend only the lower-level schools, and sometimes at different hours from the boys. In most towns, parents had to pay part of the tuition to get their young educated. These barriers to the education of all characterized the New England colonies in the Northeast as well as those in the middle-Atlantic and the South. In those sections of North America that were then governed by Spain or France, even less was done for education. Christian missionaries made intermittent efforts to evangelize Native Americans and African Americans through religious education across North America; but schooling, whether local or continental, was not primarily a governmental matter.

The Religious Roots of Colonial Schooling

However, in spite of patchwork, casual customs of schooling throughout the British colonies, there was a push for literacy among many colonists, based largely on the Protestant belief that lay people should learn to read the Bible in the vernacular tongue (that is, for British colonists, in English, rather than Latin or Greek). Passing a law in 1647 for the provision of schools, the Massachusetts colonial legislature commented that "old deluder Satan" had kept the Bible from the people in the times before the Protestant Reformation, but now they should learn to read. Thus, the legislature decreed, towns of over 50 families should provide a school. They did not specify that the education had to be free, nor did they require attendance. The law was weakly enforced. In effect, parents decided whether to send their children; if they did, they had to pay part or all of the cost; and religion was without doubt or question intertwined with education in those days. The most popular schoolbook in British colonial America, *The New England Primer*, taught children their ABC's through rhymed couplets, beginning with "In Adam's Fall, We sinned all," and concluding with "Zaccheus he Did climb the Tree, Our Lord to see."

Schools offered brief terms, perhaps six weeks in winter and another six weeks in summer, attended mainly by young children who were not working in the fields. These practices swayed to the rhythms of agricul-

tural work and the determination of most towns to provide only modest resources for schools. Formal schooling was more extensive for a tiny elite, as it was in
America's parent country, England. In the colonies, only
a few boys of European ancestry might go on to more
advanced schools for English grammar and then, for an
even smaller number, tutoring in Latin, leading to Harvard College, or Yale, or William and Mary. The majority
of these privileged few then became ministers, rather
than leaders in secular society.

The rest of the children learned most of their literacy, adult roles, work skills, and traditions outside of
school, from a constellation of institutions, principally
the home, the workplace, and the church. However, as
colonial society became more highly populated, more
complex, and more riven by faction in the 18th century,
competition among rival Protestant denominations and
quarrels developed over religious doctrine. In addition,
political and financial issues ultimately brought relations between the colonists and the English homeland
to a breaking point. Thus, the uses of literacy for argu-
mentation—both in oral and written form—grew. And
as agriculture became more commercial and efficient, it
brought more cash transactions, more focus on single
crops, and the prospect of more distant markets, into
the countryside, reinforcing the value of literacy. In the
growing coastal towns of Boston, New York, Philadelphia, and Charleston, and in some inland centers like
Albany and Hartford, philanthropic groups and
churches, responding to the increase in poverty and its

visibility, established free schools for the moral education of poor children, on the model of English "charity" schools.

The Common School Movement

Given these 18th-century dynamics, one might have expected that when the colonists' victory over British forces in the American Revolution finally left newly-minted Americans free to establish republican institutions to their liking, schools would have been high on the list. Indeed, many of the Revolution's leaders thought they should be—including Thomas Jefferson and Benjamin Rush. Jefferson wrote from France in 1786, advising a friend to "preach a crusade against ignorance," and support free schools in Virginia. Rush, a Philadelphia physician and signer of the Declaration of Independence, proposed a similar bill for free schools in Pennsylvania.

Leaders of this movement for state systems of common schools in the early national period came from both the Jeffersonian Republicans and the Federalists. But their efforts failed in their state legislatures. Most free citizens, it appears, thought that the patchwork colonial mode of education was still quite sufficient. In particular, Americans were wary of any increase in taxes (which had been a major point of contention with England) and did not want their fledgling state governments to meddle in affairs that had always been local matters for towns or families to decide. After Jefferson's bill for free schools in the Virginia legislature had failed twice, he complained to his friend Joel Barlow in 1807, "There is a snail-paced gait for the advance of new ideas on the general mind, under which we must acquiesce."

Thus, in the countryside, towns still decided whether to have a school, and if so, how to fund it. The cost was usually covered through some combination of taxes on all citizens plus tuition fees for the parents of children who attended. Sometimes parents paid by providing food for the teacher or firewood for the school, but usually it was cash. Parental payments were called "rate bills." Sometimes the school would be free for all children for a set amount of time and then a "continuation" school would be provided for those whose parents were able to pay. Thus the amount of schooling a child received was in the last analysis determined by wealth. At most, there would be a single school for each town or district. Blacks and Indians in general received no formal schooling in these institutions. Even for white children, the terms were brief, the teachers often poorly educated, and the buildings generally in poor condition. The rural school became a favorite target of school reformers later in the early 19th century. Michigan's superintendent, John Pierce, called little rural districts "the paradise of ignorant teachers"; another report spoke of a district school building in such bad repair that "even the mice had deserted it."

The Monitorial School Model

In cities, there were more opportunities. Even in the 18th century in urban areas, there were several different kinds of schools, funded in different ways and with different levels of financial resources. A modest amount of "charity" schooling provided some free instruction for children of poor whites and of African Americans, often subsidized by churches and by state and local government. Such efforts resulted in African Free Schools, "infant" schools for the two- and three-year-old children of the indigent, and other types of sponsorship. As time passed and as concern grew, many cities in the new Republic experimented with a type of charity school, the "monitorial" school, which became popular in England, Europe, and Latin America in the 1810s and '20s. Invented by Joseph Lancaster, a Quaker schoolmaster in England, the "monitorial" school model encouraged more advanced pupils to teach those who were less advanced. Lancaster wrote many manuals in his efforts to popularize the methods. Lancaster attempted to define appropriate discipline and to provide detailed instructions for classroom procedures. At a time when boys were routinely paddled for school infractions, advocates applauded Lancaster's ideas about motivation without corporal punishment, discipline motivated by an active curriculum and competition, neutrality with regard to religious denominations, and, perhaps most important, economy of expense. Lancaster claimed that with his system a single master could teach 500 poor children at a time. By the 1820s, Lancasterian schools had popped up in Pittsburgh, Harrisburg, and many other Pennsylvania towns; in Detroit, Michigan; Washington, D.C.; Hartford and New Haven, Connecticut; Norfolk and Richmond, Virginia; and dozens of other cities. In New York City and in Philadelphia, reformers organized entire networks of Lancasterian monitorial schools, systems that became the physical and organizational basis of the later public free schools of those cities. Later critics derided the monitorial schools for regimenting their poor students and separating them from other children, but Lancaster's ideas helped popularize the notion of a school "system," referring not only to the pedagogy and curriculum but to the organization of schools into a network.

For parents with a bit more money, there were inexpensive pay schools advertised in the newspapers, taking in children whose parents could afford a few shillings a quarter. The wealthy educated their children with private tutors or sent them to expensive boarding schools in the English style, now increasingly available to the English-speaking ex-colonials. The cream of society might even send their favored sons and daughters to acquire intellectual and social finesse in academies abroad. Well into the 1820s and '30s, "free" education thus connoted only limited privileges granted to the poor, and was distinctly dependent on the goodwill of local congregations, both Protestant and Catholic, or perhaps the largesse of nondenominational philanthropic societies. In New York and elsewhere these charity schools might receive some support, variously from the city council or the state. Our current distinction between "private" and "public" education had not yet crystallized.

The Common School Reform Movement Gathers Steam

Meanwhile, in the small towns and countryside, where a majority of Americans still lived, school reformers of the 1840s worked to end the discriminatory practices of continuation schools and rate bills, recommending instead that schools be supported entirely by property taxes. In effect, this meant that all property owners would subsidize education for the entire community. Traditional opponents of taxation labeled this an unwarranted and oppressive intrusion of state government into local affairs; however, Henry Barnard, Connecticut's school superintendent, called it "the cardinal idea of the free school system." Reformers also urged the centralization of the little rural districts into larger town-wide units, for better supervision and support. Simultaneously, in urban settings, school reformers of the same period began to focus their efforts on absorbing the charity schools into free public school systems and then trying to attract the children of more affluent parents into these "common" schools. The idea of the school as a common, equal meeting ground took on great force for reformers, and they aimed their criticisms at the evils of private schools. A system of private

60

schools for the rich, said Orville Taylor in 1837, "is not republican. This is not allowing all, as far as possible, a fair start." The present system, Henry Barnard complained, "classifies society...assorting children according to the wealth, education, or outward circumstances of their parents." As Jefferson had discovered earlier, however, old practices die hard. Even Horace Mann, the best known of the education reformers in the 1840s, lamented the slow progress of his efforts, labeling his opponents as "an extensive conspiracy" of "political madmen."

There remained much support for small-scale district control. In Massachusetts, for example, traditional Protestants of the Congregational denomination rightly perceived that the state would use its influence to discourage the advocacy of particular doctrines in such common schools. In New York state, a petition from a little town in Onondaga County complained that the newly passed school law of 1849 allowed people "to put their hands into their neighbors' pockets" to get support for schools. Roman Catholics in New York City fought the creation of a single public school system, arguing that it would be biased toward Protestant beliefs. Thus, in many states, opponents of the reforms enacted in the first part of the 19th century won repeal in state legislatures and in municipal councils of key elements. In some states, the centralization of districts into towns went through waves of passage and repeal. In 1842, opponents of reform abolished the position of state superintendent of instruction in Connecticut. The Hartford

Times, a Democratic paper, called such centralized power "despotic" and "Prussian." Similar attempts to abolish the job of state superintendent failed narrowly in Massachusetts and Ohio.

Nonetheless, during the 15-year period from 1838 to 1853, most states in the Northeast (from Maine down the coast to Maryland) and the "old" Northwest (Ohio, Indiana, Illinois, Iowa, Michigan, and Wisconsin) authorized the position of state school superintendent and required towns to provide totally free schools through property taxes. What had happened between the generation of Jefferson and the generation of Horace Mann to tip the balance? We should look first at the country's economic development.

The Industrial Revolution, spawned by the cotton gin and the widespread development of steam engines, for one, had fueled further European immigration into the United States, a sprawling, crowded urbanization, and the differentiation of the economic functions of the country's three main regions in the three decades before 1860. The Midwest became an agricultural powerhouse, as well as a processing and shipping region, spawning new cities and rail transportation. Since the region's labor force was free of slavery, new European immigrants moved into the Midwest en masse. In the Northeast, agriculture, often based on small farms and in hilly country with rocky soil, became less profitable, while factory production, particularly of textiles and shoes, absorbed more and more of the labor force and dotted the landscape with new conglomerations of brick industrial towns and cities. The South, with its slave labor force and its staple crops of cotton, tobacco, and rice, remained largely rural in the decades leading up to the Civil War that would finally put an end to slavery.

It would be an oversimplification, however, to say that as economies developed, "common" schools flourished entirely as a result. Each stage contributed to progress, and each threatened to provoke a backlash. In particular, the arrival of many Roman Catholics from Ireland and Germany among the immigrants to the northern United States in the 1830s and '40s sparked a renewed chapter in the long history of Protestant-Catholic conflict, creating anxieties among leading groups of Protestants, who became persuaded that they should set aside their own denominational tensions and doctrinal disputes, at least in the education arena, while putting forward a program of moral education and a view of history that would support their values. In order to do this, the American elite and the Protestant majority had to be in favor, essentially, of centralized schooling, and they had to abandon some traditions of rural independence, cultural separatism, and local control.

The Role of the Whig Party

The political party that best represented progressive Protestantism in the three decades prior to the Civil War was the Whig Party. Born in the 1820s, the Whig Party as time went on increasingly based its politics on government activism that included programs of institution building, economic development, and moral regulation—resulting in canals, insane asylums, temperance societies whose purpose was to discourage alcohol abuse, and free public schools. Most of the early state superintendents of public instruction of the 1840s were Whigs, and most of the laws to create the first school systems were Whig-sponsored.

There was some bipartisan support, to be sure. Many Democrats also supported free education for all and wanted schools to teach children morals, the glories of America's past, and the virtues of its political institutions. Yet it fell to the Democratic Party of the day to favor local control and oppose strong state government intervention. Criticizing this view, Whig leader William Seward, the governor of New York, said it was absurd to think that a nation could employ its resources in carrying on war, punishing crime, and fighting sedition but could not employ the same resources to "avert the calamities of war, provide for the public security, prevent sedition, improve the public morals, and increase the general happiness."

It was a hard-fought battle. But in a relatively short period, from 1837 to 1853, every state legislature in the North passed into law most of the key features of common free school systems. To prevail in these hard-fought battles, common school advocates, working largely through the Whig Party, had to convince a majority of their compatriots that common schools could play a critical role, not just in providing people a more equal chance at education, but in consolidating the country's culture around republican, capitalist, and Protestant values.

In the South, a regionally strong 19th-century Democratic Party, localism, a laissez-faire tradition about education, and a strong belief in a hierarchical society based on slave labor, combined to thwart the more democratic and middle-class values of the region's school reformers. Free common schools would come to the South only in the aftermath of the 1861-65 Civil War, first introduced and promoted by the Reconstruction legislatures that included black legislators in the 1860s and early '70s. Then, in the late 19th century, when Southern white Democrats had returned to power in the state legislatures, the region gradually moved toward free school systems based on property taxes, but separate for blacks and whites and unequal in their resources. Indeed, there was much racial segregation in the North as well, and schools for racial minorities across the nation generally had poorer resources.

The Balance Wheel of the Social Machinery

As the modern common school system began to acquire a clear shape in the North between 1837 and 1853, it retained evolutionary, rather than revolutionary, features. Governance, while devolved from strictly local groups, was still shared between local and state authorities, with increasing federal involvement in the 20th century. The amount of control retained to this day by local, elected school boards in the United States is unique among the industrial nations of the world, and testifies to how dearly the concept of local control of school curricula and of their budgets still appeals to the average American. However, by introducing a modicum of state regulation, and in persuading local school districts to remove all parental fees for children's school attendance, the common school reformers affected a significant shift. Class bias was ameliorated if not eliminated. The ground was prepared for some integration by race. Both sexes were ultimately seen as entitled to equal educational opportunity.

Horace Mann declared in 1848 that in America, common, public schools would be "the balance wheel of the social machinery," and the idea of equality of opportunity—in many senses implicit in the texts of the Declaration of Independence and in the U.S. Constitution—was reinforced and expanded by that declaration, and similar reformist credos. However, the balance wheel metaphor has another, perhaps unintended meaning. A balance wheel keeps machinery from shaking apart. This is what has kept public schools attractive to most of the public in most parts of the country for the past century and a half. Americans have consistently believed that common public schools are necessary to teach common values, common knowledge of the political system, respect for institutions, respect for property, and other values that are needed to keep a democratic system from flying apart. Thus, while promoting equality, public schools in the United States are seen by some as essentially conservative social institutions that continue some level of traditional cultural distinctions on the base of race, class, and even talent within a democratic framework. The retention of local control and the reliance on local taxes to this day creates inequalities in per-pupil expenditures. Organization of school districts along residential neighborhood lines has continued racial separatism in public education, in spite of massive attempts on the part of the federal judiciary to change this over the past half century. And very large public schools practice a certain amount of sub-organization aimed at recognizing scholarly aptitude.

To this day, the values and the curriculum of the "common" public schools remain skewed towards the cultural institutions and beliefs of traditional American Protestants. Nonetheless, as promoters of the "melting pot" concept of assimilation, public schools remain popular. Even over the past few decades, which have seen new waves of immigration from developing nations, American public schools have consistently enrolled about 90 percent of the school-age population, with the remainder largely in Roman Catholic and Protestant private schools at their own expense.

Nonetheless, as more and more Americans coming from vastly divergent ethnic and cultural backgrounds enter the public schools, some parents and educators have questioned the very idea of a single, comprehensive public school system. The heart of the debate at the moment is whether schooling conceived of in the 19-century model is preparing young Americans adequately to compete in the global technological economy of the 21st century, and if not, why not.

Americans are revisiting the issues of the great common school debates again. Should public funds be distributed directly to parents to use as they wish for their child's education? Should public funds be used for religiously based schools? Should the line between the public and private sector be blurred, as it was in the first 50 years of the nation's history? Should local and independent schooling initiatives prevail, unregulated by state and federal policy? Should there be expanded national testing within the current framework to prod lagging public school districts into providing better education for their students? A rapidly evolving society holds the answers to the current great common school debate in the United States.

Carl F. Kaestle is a professor of education, history, and public policy at Brown University. He joined the faculty at Brown in July of 1997, after teaching at the University of Wisconsin and the University of Chicago. His writings include Pillars of the Republic: Common Schools and American Society, 1780-1860, *and* Literacy in the United States: Readers and Reading Since 1880. *Recently he was a principal consultant and professional commentator in the public television documentary "School."*

5

The Sherman Anti-Trust Act of 1890

In 1890, the United States pioneered competition law and significantly strengthened the future of free markets in the American system by adopting a new federal statute: the Sherman Anti-Trust Act. For the first time in history, a national government had taken responsibility to investigate and, if necessary, prosecute monopolies and price-fixing cartels. Over time, the results of this act, denounced by captains of industry at the time of its passage, would become clear. By limiting a business's ability to dominate its competitors in the marketplace, the new law made the American economic system more dynamic and more open to new competitors and new technologies. The next century saw great economic expansion and heightened living standards in the United States.

❖ ❖ ❖

The U.S. Congress passed the statute in a time of turbulent industrial change—a time when new technologies of mass production for factory goods of all kinds were giving birth to "big business," a time when widening networks of distribution that followed the post-Civil War standardization of railroad track gauges were stitching a patchwork of regional markets together into a national economy. While these revolutionary developments presaged much greater economic efficiency than had been known in the past, at the same time, entire industries were increasingly controlled by monopolies or cartels. A cartel, it should be noted, is a group of competing companies that have agreed to set prices or take other measures to limit competition among themselves. By enacting the Anti-Trust Act to stem this behavior, Congress tipped the development of free enterprise in the American system toward competition rather than behind-the-scenes market manipulation by powerful private interests. How did Congress come to choose the policy of free competition in 1890? Does the statute retain relevancy in our own time of transition to a globalized and digitized economy? Pursuing these inquiries takes us first to the congressional debates and early court decisions interpreting the law, and then to the recent Microsoft case more than a century later. Although a great deal occurred between these two chapters of economic history, both are set in periods of tempestuous industrial change in the United States and, thus, are particularly instructive episodes of antitrust enforcement.

The Railway Problem

With few exceptions, everyday life in the latter half of the 19th century lacked the telephone, the electric light, and the automobile. Rather, it depended on the horse-drawn wagon and carriage, the kerosene lamp, as well as the new and rapidly expanding network of railroads. Indeed, there was great celebration on the day a "Golden Spike" was driven to complete the first transcontinental railroad in 1869. The idea of a single railroad stretching across the continental United States sparked the imagination of citizens used to stage coach travel and the mail service carried by relay teams of horse riders known as the Pony Express.

Other national railroad lines followed and, together with regional roads and feeder lines, they soon connected the far reaches of interstate commerce. But so many railroads were built so quickly that fierce competition erupted among them and bankruptcies soon followed. Most notably, when the great Northern Pacific Railway defaulted on debts owed to its investment bank, the bank closed its doors, precipitating the Financial Panic of 1873. The New York Stock Exchange closed for 10 days in the fall of that year because the panic threatened to collapse the stock market. As the crisis spread, almost 90 railroads defaulted on bonds, closing more banks and driving the economy into a financial crisis that persisted through the 1870s.

Nonetheless, railroad building continued. As did the difficulties. Into the 1890s, an annual average of 50 railroads were still failing. Everyone acknowledged the "railway problem," but there was no consensus on an acceptable solution.

Congress first approached the problem by passing the Interstate Commerce Act of 1887 to protect small businesses and the railroads themselves from the favorable pricing on freight shipments railroads felt compelled to grant to industrial monopolies and other powerful customers. The law prohibited railroads from engaging in price discrimination—from charging lower prices to powerful customers simply because they demanded them. Still, ferocious pressure continued. The railroads' solution to the demands of their customers was to join together in price-fixing cartels themselves. By the turn of the 20th century, the flight from competition to combination spread far beyond railroads. Giant cartels as well as corporate mergers between competitors were reshaping and consolidating industries throughout the economy—from oil refining and steel production to wooden match and crèpe paper manufacture.

The Rise of Standard Oil

The most famous example involved an accountant from northern Ohio named John D. Rockefeller. By

1859, oil had been discovered in Ontario, Canada, and in western Pennsylvania. Most crude oil from both fields was sent to refineries in northern Ohio for processing into useful forms like kerosene. In less than 15 years, Rockefeller had become an enormously successful businessman because he controlled the Ohio oil refineries and, with them, the entire industry. He used this control as leverage over the railroads, already financially weakened by their own proliferation and intense competition. Their condition allowed Rockefeller the leverage to obtain not only lower rates for transporting his Standard Oil Company products but also a portion of every dollar his rivals paid the railroads. He extracted these payments by approaching each railroad and threatening it with the loss of his business, which was quite substantial and, thus, critical in an industry whose thin profit margin made it dependent on traffic volume.

As a result, independent oil companies were crushed, many of them selling out to Standard Oil. In 1892, the Ohio attorney general won a court order to dissolve the Standard Oil Company, but Rockefeller simply moved to New Jersey, turning it into the first "trust"– a company controlling formerly independent competitors by holding their stock certificates. The old trusts were different from today's holding companies, whose stock portfolios are diversified across industries and, thus, do not raise concerns about monopoly power in particular markets.

Although few companies actually adopted the form of a "trust," the term rapidly became the catchword in public debate over the government's role in a time of such industrial concentration. Some saw increasing industrial concentration as natural and beneficial. Steel baron Andrew Carnegie said that "this overpowering irresistible tendency toward aggregation of capital and increase of size...cannot be arrested." Even the progressive-minded journalist Lincoln Steffens remarked: "Trusts are natural, inevitable growths out of our social and economic conditions. ...You cannot stop them by force, with laws."

As it became clear that states could not or would not curtail the growth of trusts of all types, Congress held hearings on how it might address the issue. In 1888, Senator John Sherman of Ohio introduced his anti-trust bill and declared:

> The popular mind is agitated with problems that may disturb social order, and among them all none is more threatening than...the concentration of capital into vast combinations. ...Congress alone can deal with them and if we are unwilling or unable there will soon be a trust for every product and a master to fix the price for every necessity of life.

Still, there were some in Congress who differed with Senator Sherman. They sided with Carnegie and Steffens as well as Rockefeller, who would later testify before the United States Industrial Commission: "It is too late to argue about the advantages of industrial combinations. They are a necessity."

In particular, the two men from Ohio—Sherman and Rockefeller—disagreed sharply over the prospect and the wisdom of turning the tide of increasing industrial concentration. Rhetorically, they were both speaking in favor of "free competition." But free competition held different meanings for them. For Senator Sherman, it signified competition free from domination by private economic power. It meant that free markets require limits on monopolies, cartels, and similar economic restraints. Rockefeller believed in competition free from government regulation and called for an absolute freedom of contract.

Thus, in 1890, social concerns about massive industrial transformation, economic concerns about the monopolies and cartels that threatened free markets, and political concerns about the fundamental "liberty of the citizen" in a nation where trusts might become very powerful motivated Congress to pass the Sherman Anti-Trust Act.

In the American system, legislation typically serves as the beginning of social change. Thereafter, laws are applied and policies interpreted by the courts, where the sharp divide between the two sons of Ohio, Sherman and Rockefeller, continued to play out for decades.

The Supreme Court Upholds the New Law

Two landmark antitrust cases involving railroads soon reached the Supreme Court, the first in 1896. In *United States v. Trans-Missouri Freight Association*, the U.S. attorney general sued a railroad cartel whose 18 members argued that they were merely setting reasonable prices to avert ruinous competition. Although the railroads' argument persuaded the lower courts, a divided Supreme Court held the cartel illegal and announced that only the competitive process could set reasonable prices. The Court majority also observed that such "combinations of capital" threatened to "driv[e] out of business the small dealers and worthy men whose lives have been spent therein." A few years later, the Court factions reaffirmed the validity of the Sherman Anti-Trust Act more clearly, uniting to declare that all price-fixing cartels were illegal:

> ...we can have no doubt that [cartels], however reasonable the prices they fixed, however great the competition they had to encounter, and however great the necessity for curbing themselves by joint agreement from committing financial suicide by ill-advised competition, [are prohibited] because they...deprive the public of the advantages which flow from free competition.

With overt price-fixing cartels clearly illegal, the railroads turned to mergers as the way to eliminate competition between them. Thus, the second landmark case to test the statute was brought by the U.S. attorney general to break up the Northern Securities Trust, the result of a merger engineered by the financier J. P. Morgan. His group had come to control the faltering Northern Pacific Railway, which competed along 9,000 miles of parallel track with the Union Pacific, amongst whose owners was Rockefeller. To end the cutthroat competition between the two railroads, Morgan persuaded the two ownership groups to merge by exchanging their railroad stock for trust certificates. The federal government brought suit to dissolve the trust.

In 1904, a bare majority of the Supreme Court approved the government action to break up the railroad trust. Four of the nine justices dissented, insisting that the merger, like any commercial contract, was simply a sale of property. For them, free competition meant the right to sell or exchange one's business free from government intervention, regardless of its actual impact on the market. The Court majority, however, insisted that free competition calls for attention to the impact on the market. Crucially, it determined that the Anti-Trust Act prohibited this particular merger because the resulting trust necessarily eliminated competition between the railroads and created a monopoly. The Court declared:

> *The mere existence of such a combination and the power acquired by the holding company as its trustee, constitute a menace to, and a restraint upon, that freedom of commerce which Congress intended to recognize and protect, and which the public is entitled to have protected. If such combination be not destroyed, all the advantages that would naturally come to the public under the operation of the general laws of competition...will be lost.*

Even as the Sherman Act played out in the railroad industry, Rockefeller's Standard Oil Trust continued to wage a relentless assault on the petroleum industry. His vision of a unified and efficient network of petroleum

production and distribution entailed a methodical program of intimidation that left his rivals with no choice
but to sell out for pennies on the dollar.

But in1902, President Teddy Roosevelt took action
that would make his reputation as a "trust-buster": On
his instruction, the U.S. attorney general filed suit to
break up Standard Oil, whose predatory conduct had
come to symbolize the entire trust problem. Court cases
can take a long time, but in 1911, the Supreme Court
finally held that Standard Oil had illegally monopolized
the petroleum industry. Simply put, its success had not
been fairly won. The result was a decree to dissolve
Standard Oil into 33 separate companies known as "baby Standards."

The Anti-Trust Act was a resounding success, or so it
seemed. Price-fixing cartels were stopped in their tracks
and the notorious Northern Securities and Standard Oil
trusts were no more. The *Washington Post* would declare on May 18, 1911, that the Supreme Court decision
"dissolves the once sovereign Standard Oil Company as
a criminal corporation. ...[H]onest men will find security
from alarms and indictments, while dishonest men will
see in it the certainty of punishment. ...[I]t has given the
country assurance of justice and progress in its industry."

But in retrospect the success was not so clear. First,
the break up of Standard Oil permitted its shareholders
to retain ownership and control of the 33 baby Standards. Thus they were not independent companies, except in name. Furthermore, in congressional hearings

several years later, evidence showed that their profits had actually increased, suggesting the break up had certainly not diminished their economic power, whatever their structure on paper had come to resemble. Yet there were others who pointed not to Rockefeller's ruthlessness but to his success in creating an efficient distribution network, and to the benefits to consumers of decreasing prices for petroleum products in those years. But in the end it was a question of competition on the merits, not competitive success by any means. Indeed, Nobel Laureate Douglass C. North has recently written that the success of free market economies depends on the belief that participants will have a fair opportunity to succeed.

Antitrust Law and the Modern Age

More recent critics of the Anti-Trust Act point to as many as five merger waves, the first beginning in the late 19th century. For example, General Motors Corporation and the now-defunct AT&T and U.S. Steel corporations resulted from mergers that successfully consolidated the automobile, telecommunications, and steel industries for the better part of the 20th century. In the critics' view, the Anti-Trust Act, in spite of its affirmation by the Court, did not reverse the trend toward industrial concentration and, with it, the increasing consolidation of economic and political power that had originally moved Congress to act in 1890. Yet since the1970s, in spite of the enormous authority and prestige of corporations in American life, the Justice Department and the Federal Trade Commission in both Republican and Democratic administrations have accepted their statutory responsibility to review all large mergers and often insisted on changes to reduce their anti-competitive effects. Indeed, the AT&T monopoly of telephone service was broken up during Ronald Reagan's first term.

Still, it is particularly hard to ignore the fact that even after a century of trust-busting, legal mergers have consolidated the oil industry into a sector now dominated by a few large multinational corporations. Indeed, the argument that concentration is good continues. Moreover, times have changed, many argue: Global competition reduces the tension between the benefits of large-scale enterprise and the harms of industrial concentration. Others insist that tensions have not lessened but rather shifted from the national to the international stage, as evidenced by disputes adjudicated by the World Trade Organization and similar groups.

Nonetheless, thanks to Senator Sherman, the commitment to prohibit price-fixing has remained resolute: In 1999, for example, the federal government concluded its case against an international vitamin cartel when its members agreed to fines approaching $1 billion and to imprisonment of the corporate managers involved. As a general matter, there is an international consensus about the economic evils of price-fixing cartels as unjustifiable restraints of competition. More than 100 countries have enacted competition laws modeled on the

Sherman Anti-Trust Act—from the European Union and its member states to Japan and Zambia.

In the United States, the Anti-Trust Act has both enunciated and strengthened an enduring commitment to opening markets to new technologies and new groups. No longer do a few wealthy businessmen like Rockefeller and Carnegie, Vanderbilt and Dupont, dominate commercial enterprise and control economic opportunity. As the 20th century progressed, the inventive energies bubbling at the core of the American economy were unleashed to create new centers of innovation and entrepreneurial activity, whether in Hollywood, on Madison Avenue, or across the Internet from California's Silicon Valley to its counterparts in the environs of Austin and Boston.

The Microsoft Case

The dialectic of concentration versus competition continues, even as it mutates into new forms. It should come as no surprise that our own time of dramatic technological and economic transformation has given rise to a second great monopolization case: Since 1990, Microsoft Corporation, the software manufacturer, has been investigated and sued by the U.S. federal government and 20 U.S. states, as well as by the European Union and numerous private plaintiffs. Notably, the Anti-Trust Act, a 19th century statute, was still at the heart of the U.S. cases seeking to curb Microsoft's allegedly anticompetitive conduct in high technology industries at the cusp of the 21st century.

Bill Gates and Paul Allen founded Microsoft in the 1970s. Allen would leave the company while Gates cultivated an image of youthful exuberance and geeky innovation. But behind Gates's public persona was a corporate strategist whose tactics of competition some have likened to those of John D. Rockefeller. Microsoft Windows is clearly the dominant operating system for personal computers (PCs) just as Standard Oil was the dominant distribution system for the petroleum industry. In the U.S. government case against Microsoft, the United States District Court in Washington, D.C., found that Microsoft retained its dominance by intimidating computer companies as powerful as Intel and IBM and as frail as Apple Computer into withholding from consumers products that had the potential to challenge Microsoft Windows software.

Various tribunals ultimately found that Microsoft illegally monopolized the major market for PC operating systems. Unlike Standard Oil, however, Microsoft was not broken up. It was ordered to cease discriminatory pricing and product access policies, and to share basic information about its Windows PC operating system needed for rivals to compete more effectively and freely with Microsoft in the market for applications software on the Windows platform.

In the European Union case, the Commission imposed similar restrictions as well as a fine of 497.2 million Euros. Microsoft settled numerous suits worldwide, both public and private, at a cost of additional billions of dollars.

As a result, the ethos of the information technology industry changed. Companies began to engage more freely in research that competes fundamentally with Microsoft technology. Indeed, Microsoft has recently embarked on a new course of patent cross-licensing that is a radical departure from its history of sharp competition. While it is too early to assess the ultimate impact of Microsoft's shift toward cooperation, what is clear is that the Sherman Anti-Trust Act has retained its legal relevance and has already had a substantial role to play in regulating the commerce of the Information Age.

Has the Anti-Trust Act made a difference in the United States over the past century? The answer is clearly yes with respect to overt price-fixing cartels and with respect to the most flagrant examples of predatory commercial monopolies. But the effect on corporate mergers and other commercial acquisitions and, thus, on industry concentration, is less certain. On the one hand, there is evidence that corporate mergers have continued to proliferate throughout the century (often failing to produce the efficiencies promised by consolidation). On the other, globalization and federal oversight in the spirit of Senator Sherman has arguably diminished their anticompetitive effects. In a nation characterized by a powerful ethos of free competition, the Sherman Act has—often successfully—mediated between two partially contradictory consequences of that ethos: a commitment to competition unfettered by excessive government regulation, and freedom from market domination by powerful private interests.

Commerce continues, but in a world that has changed. Everyday life now includes global telephone service, as well as satellite and cable radio and television. Medical research has opened new doors to improved health and increased longevity. The Internet offers fingertip access to economic goods, a medium for political voice, and instant interpersonal communication. As the 21st century unfurls, the Sherman Act will face the increasing challenge of mediating tensions between competition policy and the legal monopolies granted by patent and copyright protection, which appear to be the most important forms of wealth in the emerging information society.

Rudolph J. R. Peritz is a professor of law and director of the IProgress Project at New York Law School. He teaches courses in antitrust law, intellectual property law, contract law, cyberlaw, and jurisprudence. Before entering the legal profession, he was a software engineer and programmer for mainframe computer systems. He has been visiting professor at LUISS University, Rome, Italy, and at the University of Essex in the United Kingdom. He has written two books and numerous articles on competition law, intellectual property rights, and cyberlaw. He is currently at work on a project entitled The Political Economy of Progress.

6

The Interstate Highway System, 1939-1991

In April 1939, executives of the General Motors Corporations inaugurated a major exhibit at the New York World's Fair. Named "Futurama"—a word intended to signify a panorama of the future—the General Motors' exhibit immediately became the fair's most popular attraction. Each day—even during the sweltering summer—thousands of visitors waited in long lines to enter Futurama. Once inside, they rode in cars around a track, looking at the exhibit below that portrayed the United States as General Motors thought it might become in far-off 1960. Visitors observed farmlands described as "drenched in blinding sunlight," cities characterized as "breathtaking," and above all, highways, vast river-like highways featuring smooth-flowing traffic.

❖ ❖ ❖

To wide-eyed residents of a nation still suffering the effects of the Great Depression, Futurama's designer, Norman Bel Geddes, emphasized the idea that a future of fast-flowing traffic on modern and beautifully designed, limited-access highways would help restore prosperity and hope to residents of city and countryside. Also in 1939, senior engineers at the U.S. Bureau of Public Roads came to a similar conclusion in a report issued that year entitled, *Toll Roads and Free Roads.* Like Bel Geddes, the authors of this report concluded that a new generation of urban road improvements would eliminate "properties [that] are dying," leading to "new and important developments." We now know that this unlikely convergence of a popular world's fair exhibit and a government report—as the Great Depression set the stage for World War II—set in motion long-term planning among state and federal road engineers, business leaders, and politicians that would finally result in the construction of the Interstate Highway System (IHS).

Before World War II, American engineers had constructed a limited number of freeway-like roads, including the great parkways in New York State, the Pennsylvania Toll Road, Chicago's Lake Shore Drive, and the Arroyo-Seco freeway in Los Angeles. Many of those same engineers had also studied and visited the much larger Autobahn system that was being constructed in Germany. However, in 1939, there was still no major political constituency for a grand system of highways to link the nation more tightly together. Advocates of such a system realized that securing congressional approval to finance construction of the IHS would never be automatic, or easy. Instead, those state and federal engineers who believed the nation would be better off with superhighways often took the lead in efforts to persuade political and business leaders that construction of a costly new system on top of the roads the nation already had would "pay off" for society in terms of improved traffic volume and flow, rising property values, and in particular reinvigoration of business in the nation's downtown areas.

Champion of a Highway System

Among the visionaries and planners of the era, no one was more active in promoting construction of the interstate system than Thomas H. MacDonald, chief of the U.S. Bureau of Public Roads from 1919 to 1953. Authoritative in style, and known for having clear expectations for himself and his subordinates, MacDonald was addressed respectfully by colleagues—and even by members of the U.S. Congress—as "Chief." In 1904, MacDonald had graduated from Iowa State University with a degree in civil engineering. Like all or most engineering graduates of that era, MacDonald's instructors had emphasized the importance of practical solutions for the many practical problems of constructing highways and other physical improvements such as dams, railroads, and water and sewer systems. These projects were appropriate for a nation that was welcoming vast numbers of immigrants while still expanding westward and building new towns and cities. Like other senior federal officials such as Herbert Hoover, who was secretary of commerce (1921-1928) and then president of the United States (1929-1932), MacDonald, once he assumed nationwide responsibilities for highway construction, began to contemplate construction of a highway system far grander (and far costlier) than anything he had been taught in college. The motorcar, popularized by Henry Ford only a few decades earlier, was beginning to make a large segment of the population mobile and was also fuelling economic growth.

MacDonald was a missionary for highway improvements. One of his favorite arguments was that motorists and truckers could themselves pay for better roads in the form of higher gasoline taxes that would subsidize their construction. He pointed out that car and truck drivers were already paying just as much money, or more, for the privilege of driving on antiquated highways in the form of their own lost time, lost wages, and avoidable accidents. In numerous speeches and articles, MacDonald regularly drew connections between construction of an Interstate Highway System and the promise that cities as a whole and especially the central business district would experience not only reduced traffic, but also rising property values, increased employment, and improved sales. The point was that if the majority of long-distance traffic was shunted out of towns and cities, that the downtown centers of those places would become more pleasant to live, shop, and work.

MacDonald was able to buttress his claims with impressive studies of automobile and truck traffic conducted by state road engineers. After World War II, as Americans experienced renewed prosperity, traffic in local areas grew even more miserable for truckers and motorists stuck on two-lane highways that inevitably wound through the downtown areas of every town and city on the route. In addition, retailers on these traffic-clogged main streets increasingly lost sales to competitors opening stores in distant suburbs where it was easy to build giant parking lots. MacDonald's arguments took on even greater authority and urgency. Not until 1956, however, would members of Congress vote to appropriate funds to build the IHS.

City vs. Country

In 1944, as America's leaders planned for the end of World War II, the possible Interstate Highway System was on the federal legislative agenda. Members of the U.S. Congress and President Franklin D. Roosevelt, however, could not at first agree on terms for funding postwar highway construction. One dispute was that farm groups and their many representatives in Congress wanted more federal aid to construct miles of low-cost roads that would make it easier for farmers to bring crops and families to nearby towns and markets. At the same time, representatives from New Jersey and New

York and other east coast states with large urban populations demanded additional funds to pay for roads that
would help improve traffic in congested cities. Proponents felt that federal money for highway projects
promised a vast public works program for members of
the armed forces as soon as the war ended. Truck owners, however, were not interested in whether highway
building fostered jobs or improved property values.
Leaders of the American Trucking Associations, a trade
group composed of thousands of truck fleet owners and
managers, urged reduction of gasoline taxes and construction of key routes that served shipping traffic.

Late in 1944, political leaders and leaders in the
American trucking and farm industries reached a compromise. The federal government would pay 50 percent
of the cost of building roads in cities as well as in rural
areas important to farmers. As well, Congress would
pay 50 percent of the costs to continue construction of
the original federal-aid highway system, which since
1921 had formed the backbone of U.S. highways and included such well-known routes as US 66 running from
Chicago to Los Angeles. To pay for all of that projected
postwar road building, members of Congress voted to
appropriate the then-gigantic sum of $450 million a
year for three years starting as soon as the war ended.
As part of this legislation, Congress authorized construction of the Interstate Highway System, but did not
appropriate funds specifically to pay the immense costs
for building it. Rather, Congress authorized state offi-

cials to transfer up to 25 percent of federal grants for highway construction to build the IHS.

During the late 1940s, however, few of those involved either at the federal or state level were willing to divert funds from relatively inexpensive urban and rural roads that promised to speed up traffic and get farmers to market in order to build 40,000 miles of the still untested and far more costly (per mile) Interstate Highway System. More important than engineering miracles, the $450 million appropriated by Congress promised construction contracts and jobs in every state of the union and certainly in most congressional districts. Disputes about the distribution of money—highway mileage politics, in other words—have always played an important role in shaping American highway legislation. In any event, in December 1944, President Roosevelt signed the Federal-Aid Highway Act of 1944, launching the largest and certainly the most expensive road-building program in the history of the federal government.

Postwar Traffic Jams

The legislation was fortuitous. Following the war, the nation's economy boomed, and everyone wanted a new car. Between 1945 and 1955, Americans more than doubled the number of automobiles and trucks on the nation's streets. In urban areas such as New York, Chicago, Los Angeles, Dallas, Miami, and Houston, traffic jams, delays, and accidents spiraled upward. In 1950, the U.S. Chamber of Commerce reported that 40 percent of trip time in New England cities was wasted in traffic jams. As traffic delays grew worse, downtown retailers continued to worry about lost sales to new competitors who were opening stores in fast-growing suburbs. In spite of the Federal-Aid Highway Act, rapid increases in the costs of labor and materials reduced the number of miles actually constructed. Equally important, truck and auto manufacturers built—and Americans purchased—vehicles that were heavier, faster, and longer. If road engineers such as MacDonald were to construct a new generation of roads that were safe and efficient, then those roads would also have to be wider, thicker, and far costlier to build and maintain. MacDonald estimated that the pressure of traffic on the nation's roads was eight times greater than in the decades before World War II. As in previous years, leaders of farm, truck, and urban groups remained deadlocked over who should pay for these new roads and where they should be located.

Starting in 1951, leaders of the influential trucking industry attempted to break the deadlock in highway politics. In this period, most trucking firms were small, employing only a few office personnel and fewer than 100 drivers. The key to truckers' clout in American politics was their trade association. Headquartered in Washington, D.C., and with members in every state, the American Trucking Associations (ATA) employed talented attorneys who were expert at defending truckers' interests in courts and at bringing the concerns of member truckers to the offices of senators, representatives, and to the White House. Complaining of traffic delays, truck operators still wanted the federal government to spend less money on little used rural roads and more money on key routes in and through major cities. During the period 1951-1953, they began a lobbying campaign called PAR, which stood for Project Adequate Roads. (Excellent at adapting their aims to American political culture, leaders of the ATA also understood that every golf player hoped to shoot "par," which was the score that a professional golfer would achieve on a demanding golf course). In spite of their considerable clout, not even leaders of the ATA were capable of jump-starting the Interstate Highway System.

President Eisenhower and the Clay Committee

President Dwight D. Eisenhower, who assumed office in 1953, also failed to break the deadlock over who would pay the cost of building the IHS. Like his contemporaries, Eisenhower wanted to reduce traffic jams, and in principle he supported the idea of a new highway system. Construction of the IHS over a long period of time, Eisenhower and his economic advisers believed, would help stimulate the U.S. economy. At the same time, however, Eisenhower did not want a highway funding program that would place too great a financial burden on the federal budget.

In August 1954, Eisenhower asked former U.S. Army General Lucius D. Clay to head a committee that would recommend some way of financing an Interstate Highway System. In January 1955, Clay recommended issuance by the U.S. government of $25 billion in bonds that would be retired over 30 years with funds derived from the federal tax on gasoline and occasional borrowing from the U.S. Treasury. Bond sales to corporations, governments, and private individuals, Clay reasoned, would finance most of the costs of building the IHS without adding to the federal budget or the national debt. Bowing to political reality, Clay proposed that the federal government would pay 90 percent of the costs associated with building the IHS and state governments would pay 10 percent. Up to that point, the federal and state governments had continued to split the costs of highway building on a 50-50 basis.

Immediately, Clay's plan was attacked by the same interest groups. Leaders of farm groups objected to Clay's plan to freeze spending on local farm roads for a period of 30 years while the bonds were paid off. Equally important, the powerful Senator Harry F. Byrd of Virginia did not want the federal government to have to pay interest on such a large bond issue.

As an alternative to Clay's ideas, Representative George H. Fallon of Maryland prepared legislation that would have paid directly for highway construction out of the U.S. federal budget. Fallon's bill, however, required a vast increase in gasoline and tire taxes. In July 1955, nearly 500 truckers went to the nation's capital to complain to senators and representatives about Fallon's proposal for higher taxes. On July 27, members of the House of Representatives voted to reject both Clay's proposals and the substitute offered by Fallon. Although the extremely popular President Eisenhower had narrowed the range of debate about highway funding, in this instance he could not translate that popularity into a formula that satisfied the many competitors for highway-construction dollars.

Solution to Deadlock: a Highway Trust Fund

In 1956, Senator Albert Gore Sr., of Tennessee and Representative Hale Boggs of Louisiana joined with Representative Fallon to make yet another attempt to pass IHS legislation. The key to their success was in providing a little something for all interests: more spending for rural, urban, and interstate highways, but all this accomplished with only a small increase in gasoline and other automotive and truck taxes. As part of this arrangement, Congress and Eisenhower approved creation of the Highway Trust Fund, which would designate gasoline taxes (and excise taxes on tires and trucks) for exclusive use in financing construction of the IHS and other federal-aid roads. No longer would truck operators complain about gasoline taxes used for non-highway purposes. To build public support for the final agreement, early in 1956 members of the Senate-House conference committee officially changed the name of the IHS to the National System of Interstate and Defense Highways. Ordinary Americans have called it simply the Interstate Highway System.

Finally, in 1956 Congress and the president formally conferred authority on engineers in the U.S. Bureau of Public Roads and their counterparts in the state highway departments to start the new system by building 41,000 miles, including approximately 5,000 urban miles. True to the promise of IHS enthusiasts, by the late 1980s, the compact IHS carried more than 20 percent of the nation's automobile traffic and a whopping 49 percent of the truck-trailer combinations. In the following decades, Congress approved additional mileage for the IHS, and by 2002 the rural and urban components of the total system stood at 47,742 miles. By early 2004, the federal government had spent more than $59 billion to construct urban portions of the IHS and more than $40 billion to construct the rural sections.

Protests and More Local Control

The construction of a vast new highway system affected the lives of millions of people. While many welcomed the new roads, others disliked them as symbols of runaway modernity that chewed up landscape and/or urban areas. Protests against highway building led Congress to shift control of highway construction away from state and federal engineers. As early as 1959, residents and political leaders in San Francisco blocked construction of the Embarcadero Freeway. Starting in

1962, residents of Baltimore banded together to protect city neighborhoods from destruction by highway engineers. In the late 1960s and early 1970s, upper-income residents of Northwest Washington, D.C., made use of political savvy and legal know-how to block construction of the Three Sisters Bridge across the Potomac River. Authors of books with titles such as *The Pavers and the Paved and Superhighway-Superhoax* attracted national attention to this "freeway revolt" taking place.

In response to this resistance at the local level, in 1973, Congress and President Richard M. Nixon approved the Federal-Aid Highway Act, which financed local purchase of buses and fixed rail systems with money taken from the formerly inviolable Highway Trust Fund. In 1991, Congress and President George H.W. Bush approved the Intermodal Surface Transportation Efficiency Act (ISTEA). Now, local political leaders in metropolitan planning organizations could have a say in choosing whether to spend a portion of federal and state funds on highways, public transit, bike paths, or other projects. Passage of ISTEA comprised an important element in the devolution of federal highway funds and authority from national and state engineering experts to local politicians.

The construction of the Interstate Highway System produced important consequences in the American future. The vast new ribbons of concrete helped speed up the process whereby millions of Americans moved from central cities to suburbs. By 1970, the United States was already a "suburban nation." Equally important, the system (along with the postwar development of television, public schools, and the existing network of roads) was catalytic in knitting together the economic and social outlooks of more than 290 million persons. Accents, diets, and customs became less regional, more national. Nearly as important, construction of the HIS permitted truck operators to displace the nation's railroads in competition for prompt delivery of food, furniture, refrigerators, and everything else.

While railroads still maintained their own track-beds, in effect the government had fi nanced truckers' right-of-way. In terms of political consequences, after 1970 the federal highway program was devolved to the states and localities, setting a pattern for similar attempts in areas such as social welfare spending. To this day, the Interstate Highway System remains the nation's greatest public works project. It was a successful intersection between politics and commerce; an experiment that had notable consequences for transportation, urban change, social cohesion, and the reorientation of politics and public policy in the United States.

Mark H. Rose is a professor of history at Florida Atlantic University. He is the author of more than 30 articles and several books, including: The Best Transportation System in the World: Railroads, Trucks, Airlines, and American Public Policy in the Twentieth Century, *with Bruce E. Seely and Paul Barrett. Rose is also co-editor of* Business, Politics, and Society, *a book series published by the University of Pennsylvania Press.*

7

The GI Bill of Rights

The GI Bill of Rights, officially known as the Servicemen's Readjustment Act of 1944, was signed into law on
June 22, 1944, by President Franklin D. Roosevelt. At
the time, its passage through Congress was largely un-
heralded, in part because the Normandy invasion was
under way; but also because its fundamental significance and major consequences for American society
could not have been foreseen. However, with the end of
the war in both Europe and Asia just a year later, the GI
bill's provisions would soon be quickly and fully tested.
Within a few years, the new law served to change the
social and economic landscape of the United States.

❖ ❖ ❖

Among its provisions, the law made available to World
War II veterans immediate financial support in the form
of unemployment insurance. Far more important, as it
turned out, were generous educational opportunities

ranging from vocational and on-the-job training to higher education, and liberal access to loans for a home or a business.

While there were numerous bills introduced in Congress to reward the combat-weary veterans of World War II, this particular bill had a significant sponsor. The major force behind the Servicemen's Readjustment Act of 1944 was the well-known American Legion, a private veterans advocacy group founded in 1919. The Legion, during its 25th annual convention in September 1943, initiated its own campaign for comprehensive support of veterans. It labeled the resulting ideas, crafted into one legislative proposal by the Legion's national commander Harry W. Colmery, "a bill of rights for GI Joe and GI Jane," but the proposal soon became known as the GI Bill of Rights. The term GI—the slang term for American soldiers in that war—originally stood for "Government Issue," referring to military regulations or equipment. Wedded to the idea of the "Bill of Rights" in the revered U.S. Constitution, the "GI Bill" was bound to project an appealing aura in the halls of Congress as politicians sought ways to reward the homebound soldiers.

But there is more to the story. Though it might appear that the adoption and passage of the bill was entirely the result of unbridled generosity on the part of a grateful Congress, it was also in large measure a product of justified concern, even a certain fear, on the part of lawmakers about a radicalized postwar America. Prior to World War II, America had provided benefits and care to those disabled by combat, but had paid little attention to its able-bodied veterans. Within living memory of many public men of the time, neglect of the returning veterans of World War I, exacerbated by deteriorating economic conditions, had led to protest marches and disastrous confrontations. In 1932, 20,000 veterans gathered in Washington, D.C., for a "bonus march," hoping to obtain financial rewards they thought they had been promised for service in World War I, leading to one of America's most tragic moments. Altercations led President Hoover to call out the army, which under the leadership of future military heroes General Douglas MacArthur and Majors Dwight Eisenhower and George Patton used guns and tanks against the "bonus army."

In the minds of Washington policymakers who had witnessed this confrontation, the viable legislation to meet the needs of veterans that emerged in 1944 came not a moment too soon. Even when it was clear that the Allies were going to win, few foresaw the complete capitulation of the Axis powers one year later with the dropping of the atomic bomb on Hiroshima and Nagasaki, and the sudden return of more than 15 million veterans of the Army, the Navy, and the Marine Corps, streaming home from the Atlantic and Pacific theaters.

We must remember that for 12 years prior to the Japanese bombing attack on the U.S. naval base in Pearl Harbor, Hawaii—the attack that drew America into World War II—America was in a deep economic depression. Thus, the war, when it came, found the nation unprepared and largely uneducated, faced with the need to build a fighting force of young people who had known only the Great Depression years. Unemployment was widespread, with 25 percent of the workforce unemployed at the height of the depression in 1933. Breadlines and soup kitchens for even formerly prosperous middle-class men personified the era, and entire families thought they faced a life of poverty and joblessness. Most of the industrialized world in one way or another was caught up in the same calamity, with disastrous political results, including the rise of totalitarian regimes in crisis-ridden nations around the world.

Though the New Deal government of President Franklin D. Roosevelt, first elected in 1932, initiated numerous governmental programs that generated some employment, 10 million people, or about 17 percent of the workforce, were still unemployed in 1939. The outbreak of the war in Europe in 1939 brought forth a new surge of economic activity as well as an ensuing military draft. Ironically, it was the American entry into the war in late 1941 that put an end to the Great Depression, by taking young men temporarily out of circulation as most went into the military and putting everyone else to work on the home front, including large numbers of women. The American Legion, strongly supported by William Randolph Hearst and his chain of newspapers, waged their campaign for the GI Bill by stressing fear of a return to prewar breadlines and resulting threats to democracy.

Same Rules for All

In spirit, as well as specific provisions, the GI Bill was enormously democratic. Benefits were available to every veteran upon his release from active service. The rules were the same for everyone. The only requirements were military service for at least 90 days, and an honorable discharge. No financial means tests were applied, no complex tax credits had to be computed, and, most important, no preferences were given for military rank or service experiences. Length of service was used to apply only to duration of educational benefits. Minimal bureaucratic red tape was imposed for the use of any benefit.

The end of World War II was a time of great drama and release for the nation as a whole. Naturally, few people, including many closely connected to the GI Bill's development, were aware of the implications of this revolutionary new law. Commentary of the time—inside and outside of Congress—tended to stress the costs and benefits of the unemployment readjustment allowance contained in the bill and to underestimate the education and loan program provisions. The readjustment allowance authorized $20 a week of unemployment funds for 52 weeks—and soon became known to its beneficiaries as the "52-20 Club." Because of the Great Depression, few in the age group of typical GIs had ever held a job. Skeptics in and out of government said that the giveaway of $20 a week would lead to irresponsible idleness. Opposition arose in Congress from some southern members who resisted providing that much money on an equal basis to blacks and whites. In the mid-1940s, $20 was a lot of money. For 15 cents or even less, one could buy gasoline, cigarettes, beer, milk shakes, or go to a movie. Yet—and this is indicative of that generation's response to the war's end, and the stigma in those days that came with accepting public money—only slightly more than half the veterans even claimed the money; and most used it for so few weeks that less than 20 percent of the estimated cost was actually spent.

For educational benefits, the method was for the Veterans Administration (VA) to certify eligibility, pay the bills to the school for tuition, fees, and books, and to mail a monthly living stipend to the veteran for up to 48 months of schooling, depending upon length of service. For home loans for GIs, the VA guaranteed a sizeable portion of the loan to the lending institution and mortgage rates were set at a low 4 percent interest. The formal aspects of these programs have lived on in subsequent, though less generous, versions of the GI Bill for Korean War and Vietnam War veterans—and still continue as an enlistment incentive for America's current volunteer military under what is now known as the Montgomery GI Bill.

A Boost to Education

However, it was the original bill that changed everything. First among the lasting legacies of the GI Bill of Rights is the now commonplace belief that education can be and should be available to anyone, regardless of age, sex, race, religion, or family status. High school graduation was a rare achievement prior to World War II. Millions of members of the armed forces had not even graduated from grammar school and many young Americans did not go beyond the 10th grade. In the 1940s, only 23 percent of the military had a high school diploma and about 3 percent had college degrees. By making it possible for the sons of farmhands and laborers to get a better education than they had ever dreamed of, the GI Bill gave widespread and permanent credence to the idea that education is the pathway to a better job and a better life.

In 1940, a total of about 160,000 people in the United States earned college degrees. Thanks to the bill, the graduating class of 1950 numbered nearly 500,000. Importantly, these were not teenagers going to college. About half the college-student military veterans of that generation were married, and 25 percent had children. In addition to the eventual total of 2.2 million World War II veterans who attended college, another 3.5 million vets made use of vocational school opportunities, 1.5 million used it for on-the-job training, and 700,000 took farm training. The veteran chose any school or training program to which he could gain admission. Dependents of servicemen killed in action could also use the benefits. And GI educational benefits were available abroad as well. In 1950, the Veterans Administration reported that 5,800 veterans were studying in 45 countries under the GI Bill. In admitting battle-scarred vets back to civilian life, most campuses took cognizance of any educational training taken by many GIs while in service. The American Council on Education, the umbrella organization for all sectors of higher education, developed a guide for evaluating military experiences, so that suitable credits could be awarded to help speed the vet through college more quickly and then into the civilian workforce.

Not only did the GI Bill make access to higher education practical for men from all backgrounds, it changed the meaning of higher education in public consciousness from the 1950s onward. Prior to the war, higher education in the United States was mostly private, liberal arts, small-college, rural, residential, elitist, and often discriminatory from institution to institution with respect to race and religion. Today, opposites of those words provide better characterizations of higher education in the United States. American universities are now overwhelmingly public (80 percent of enrollments), focused heavily on occupational, technical, and scientific education, huge, urban-oriented, suitable for commuter attendance, and highly democratic. Now, upward social, educational, and financial mobility, rather than certification of the upper classes, is what American higher education offers to Americans and increasingly to others in the world. The resulting technological miracles in computing, in industry, medicine, and space can be attributed to a continuing stream of educated men and women.

A Flood of Veterans on Campus

Few of the minds behind the GI Bill could have envisioned the enormous enthusiasm of that generation of young men when they understood the significance of the education provisions. Few colleges and universities were prepared for the numbers of veterans who appeared to register. None were prepared for wives and children of students, a phenomenon never before experienced. Many major state universities doubled or tripled their enrollments in one or two years. University administrators felt the need to perform miracles as they faced huge lines of students, overflowing classrooms, and overworked faculty and staff. Campuses sprouted makeshift dormitories, prefabricated huts developed for the military that now held classrooms instead, and even trailer camps. Around many campuses there was the constant turmoil and noise of construction. The impact upon the surrounding communities was dramatic in terms of spurs to local business and housing development, an impact that only grew stronger in many locations over the coming decades as colleges and universities amassed more resources and prestige.

By the time initial GI Bill eligibility for World War II veterans expired in 1956—about 11 years after final victory—the United States was richer by 450,000 trained engineers, 240,000 accountants, 238,000 teachers, 91,000 scientists, 67,000 doctors, 22,000 dentists, and more than a million other college-educated individuals.

These college graduates raised expectations throughout the country, and their skilled labor contributed to a burgeoning and literate technological middle class. There was no going back to the old America dominated by agriculture and by life in small towns. College attendance, increasingly followed by careers in urban areas, became an expectation for many thereafter. By the early 1970s, one in five Americans had a college education, compared to one in 16 prior to the war. In 2004, more than 16 million Americans were enrolled in institutions of higher education, including community colleges. Currently, 1.1 million students earn bachelor's degrees each year in an American institution and an equal number earn graduate and professional degrees.

A Catalyst for Social Change

Most important, the GI Bill was one force leading to enormous social change. Settled views regarding sex, religion, and race were shaken up. Not only did the bill expose ordinary people to liberal social concepts through higher education, it led to a great mixing of different groups on campus.

Though many women had entered factories or done other kinds of work during World War II, the postwar experience of high marriage rates, sharply increased birthrates, and new opportunities for home ownership led to a home-centered role for women for the next two decades. About 64,000 of the 350,000 women veterans of World War II took advantage of the bill's higher-education opportunities, but at the time preference was largely for men and many women's colleges even went coed to accommodate the sudden spurt of enrollment. But once the opportunity had been made available, the sons and daughters of the vets (the so-called "baby boomers" born in the 1950s and '60s) went on to higher education in greater numbers. Today in the United States more women than men attend colleges and universities.

In the democratic euphoria that followed the war, many Americans reassessed their prewar prejudices. Jewish veterans gained entry into many fine schools previously known to reject or apply strict quotas for Jewish applicants, and they, as well as Catholics, benefited from the growth of public institutions in urban areas. The GI Bill helped move these children of European immigrants into academe, business, and the professions, and thus essentially eliminated religious bigotry in American higher education.

Historically black institutions of higher education experienced sharp increases in enrollments and were granted federal funds for expansion of campus construction. In northern urban areas, black veterans of the war attended formerly all-white institutions. Still, the United States was a racially segregated society in the 1940s, a pattern that continued in many regions in the 1950s. The military services were segregated (until President Truman issued a desegregation order in 1948), as were the schools in 17 states and the District of Columbia. Many black veterans were turned away from overly crowded black institutions and yet could not attend white southern schools. It took several years and another generation to accomplish what the GI Bill could not; but the foundation and development of a black middle class was a highlight of that postwar generation.

Not everyone wanted to go to college. During the war, the military had done an excellent job teaching a wide array of subjects, from reading to engineering, to millions of men from varied backgrounds. Thus motivated, many veterans obtained a high school diploma through the General Educational Development Testing Service of the American Council on Education, still known as the GED. Others continued on in vocational training schools in electronics, medical services, or business schools. Employers were encouraged to continue training their own workers with the help of the GI Bill, thereby facilitating movement into the working mainstream. Many then continued their education, establishing a grand tradition of continuous lifelong learning.

A Nation of Homeowners

This was the second durable legacy of the GI Bill. It turned the American people as never before into stakeholders, self-reliant property owners, owners of homes and businesses prepared to take responsibility for their communities because they now owned a piece of it. The dramatic impact of the GI Bill on the physical, geographic, and economic landscape of the nation is as important a legacy as the educational benefits.

It is hard to imagine the extent of the housing crisis and the pent-up consumer demand for all the necessities of life after 16 years of depression and war. It was not just the whole lack of new housing, but also that existing homes had fallen into disrepair. Even as some building resumed right after World War II, materials from nails to shingles were in short supply. Homebuilders had to compete with those building the stores and office buildings needed to restart the economy. The increasing urbanization of the nation, with most jobs concentrated in large cities, made the housing problem acute in major metropolitan areas. But the GIs returning home after years away were determined to make up for lost time by marrying, raising a family, and, of course, finally owning a home of their own, a potent symbol of economic and psychological security.

Assembly-line manufacturing techniques were applied to the building of homes. By the end of 1947, the Veterans Administration guaranteed well over one million home, business, and farm loans. Housing starts jumped from 114,000 in 1944 to 1.7 million by 1950. By 1950, the Veterans Administration guaranteed loans for over two million homes.

The "VA Loan," as it was called, meant that the government co-signed about half of a veteran's mortgage. This encouraged developers to build, bankers to lend, and veterans to buy, often with no down payment. The resulting explosion in consumer demand stirred the spirit of American manufacturers, entrepreneurs, and local officials who built new roads, schools, churches, and shopping centers. Manufacturers created or re-created in postwar style every conceivable household item to fi ll those new shopping centers and homes. Since the inception of the GI Bill and similar laws that followed, 16 million veterans have purchased homes using VA loans. Today, nearly 70 percent of the American people own their own homes.

A Decentralized Market Approach

The third legacy of the GI Bill devolved from the manner in which it was administered and funded. Under the terms of the statute, the administration of the program was concentrated in the Veterans Administration (now known as the Department of Veterans Affairs) rather than scattered government agencies or private institutions. It was a centralized federal program that was based on a decentralized market approach. Congress chose to fund the GI Bill educational benefi ts through the veterans themselves over the protests of the educational establishment, which had initially hoped and sought entirely to control the postwar allocation of such resources. This approach established the basic postwar 16 million method for subsequent federal loans and grants to college students. To this day in the United States, funds targeted at educational opportunity, such as student loans, still go directly to the student and not the institution. Similarly, the postwar housing crisis was addressed through individual loan guarantees rather than government-built and -managed housing projects, many of which have not served well in efforts to solve subsequent housing crises.

In retrospect, the GI Bill may appear to some to have been a huge public "welfare" program. But it would be wrong to think of it that way. As initially administered, it was a special law for a very special time, made available only to one generation of veterans and unrelated to need. But it has had a lasting legacy through continued application of its major themes for all veterans of wars subsequent to World War II and still serves as an inducement to sustain a volunteer military force. For non-veterans, and indeed for the nation, it established a model framework for achievement through education and property ownership. In addition, it helped create a climate where intellectual ambition became a commonplace among Americans of all backgrounds, leading to greater social tolerance, and far greater demand for a wide variety of choices, both in the consumer sphere and in other ways of living.

What the GI Bill represented, whether intended or not, is that a clear national commitment to upward mobility for a heterogeneous population pays enormous dividends for both individuals and the nation. The GI Bill enabled the nation to overcome years of instability, restored the nation's human, economic, and social capital, and helped catapult the United States to leadership on the world's stage.

Milton Greenberg is professor emeritus of government at American University in Washington, D.C., where he also served as provost and interim president. His academic career includes service on the faculties of the University of Tennessee and Western Michigan University, as dean of the College of Arts and Sciences at Illinois State University, and as vice president for academic affairs at Roosevelt University. He is co-author (with Jack C. Plano) of a major reference work, The American Political Dictionary, *first published in 1962 and now in its 11th edition. In 1997, he authored* The GI Bill: The Law That Changed America.

8

The Marshall Plan: A Strategy That Worked

It didn't start as a plan, and some of the veterans said it never did become a plan. Its own second-in-command, Harlan Cleveland, called it "a series of improvisations...a continuous international happening." Yet the European Recovery Plan (ERP)—better known as the Marshall Plan—has entered into history as the most successful American foreign policy project of all since World War II. After the fall of apartheid, South Africans called for a Marshall Plan. After the fall of the Berlin Wall, East Europeans and Russians demanded the Marshall Plan they had been denied by the Soviet Union in 1947. Fearful of disintegration in Africa, the British government in 2005 proposed coordinated international intervention on the lines of the Marshall Plan. The myth of the Marshall Plan has become as forceful as its true historical legacy.

❖ ❖ ❖

In 1955 the plan's official historian noted how, from a one-paragraph "suggestion" by Secretary of State George Marshall at a Harvard graduation ceremony, had sprung a program which "evolved swiftly into a vast spirited international adventure: as the enterprise unfolded it became many things to many men." Fifty years later, such was the fame of the project, that the same could still be said.

The Inception of an Idea

Three contingent developments led to the creation of a special new American project to help Western Europe in the spring of 1947. The first was the physical condition of the post-World War II continent after the setbacks caused by the extreme winter of 1946-47. Second was the failure of the recent Truman Doctrine—an outspoken scheme to help Greece and Turkey fight Soviet pressures—to indicate a constructive way forward for all. Third was the grueling experience of Secretary of State George Marshall in the Moscow Conference of Foreign Ministers, dedicated to the future of Germany, in March-April 1947.

Marshall had been recalled to become secretary of state by President Harry S Truman at the beginning of 1947, after retiring from the Pentagon at the end of the war as Army chief of staff. Marshall's success in that job—Churchill called him "the organizer of victory"— and his personal qualities of incisiveness, integrity, and self-abnegation made him one of the most authoritative public figures of the era. His patience and sense of duty were tested to the full in Moscow. A senior American diplomat, George Kennan, summarized Marshall's pithy conclusion upon leaving the Soviet capital:

Europe was in a mess. Something would have to be done. If he (Marshall) did not take the initiative, others would.

Kennan and his new State Department "Policy Planning Staff" produced one of the master-documents from which the Marshall Plan eventually flowed. In part, their thinking derived from Roosevelt-era understandings of the causes of two world wars and the Great Depression: class hate, poverty, backwardness, and the lack of hope for change. It was a key intention of the people in Washington rebuilding the world after the war to support the ordinary citizen's demand for a share in the benefits of industrialism. People with prosperity, or at least the prospect of it, didn't turn to totalitarianism, they believed.

But there was a specific European dimension to the Marshall effort, which came from the same reflections. Europe's evil genie, said people like Kennan, Assistant Secretary of State Dean Acheson, and future ERP Ambassador Averell Harriman, was nationalism. If that root of Nazi-fascism and all the rivalries of the 1930s could be bottled up in an integrated economic framework, uniting all the Old World, then prosperity might stand a chance, and Europe's urge to start world wars and then drag America into them might finally be killed off.

117

In these ways, modernization and integration became the twin watchwords of the ERP, and the arguments turned round how to bring them about. It was central to the method of the Marshall Plan that the Europeans should think and act for themselves within the vision: That was what made the plan not just another aid program.

In Marshall's brief and outwardly simple comments at Harvard, in June 1947, there were, first of all, explanations of Europe's devastation and hopelessness. There were warnings for those who sought to exploit the misery politically. There was a clear signal that ideology (at that point in history, Communism) should not count in reconstruction. Then came the crux of the speech, a tantalizing paragraph inviting the Europeans to agree together on what they needed and what they might do were the United States to step in. The U.S. role, Marshall said, "should consist of friendly aid in the drafting of a European program and of later support of such a program so far as it may be practical for us to do so." The secretary of state insisted that the Europeans must act jointly, and that "a cure and not a palliative" must be sought. He concluded by urging his fellow Americans to "face up to the vast responsibility which history has clearly placed upon our country."

"We expected them to jump two inches and they've jumped six feet," wrote one American journalist. In less than two weeks, the French and British foreign ministers set in motion in Paris a Conference on European Economic Cooperation (CEEC), which, in stages between the end of June and the end of September, with the help of 14 other governments, prepared a report to the State Department on the total economic aid they thought they needed. Most of those represented did not have a national plan and some not even an overall picture of their nation's economy. With no experience of any sort in joint, continent-wide planning, the delegates arrived at a grand total of $28 billion. The figure was rejected immediately by Washington as hopelessly optimistic.

But the Paris CEEC event was most famous for the arrival—and swift departure—of a large Soviet delegation headed by the Kremlin's foreign minister, Vyacheslav Molotov. In this still-controversial crisis of Cold War history, the Russians were confronted with the Western proposal for a jointly formulated and implemented recovery strategy treating the whole of Europe, including Germany, as a single economic entity. As anticipated in Washington, they walked out, insisting that the Americans and their key allies had no other intention than to line up Europe's economies under their own control and launch a new world division of labor: great power imperialism in its latest, American, guise. Soviet pressure on East European nations intensified after the rupture among the World War II allies. In February 1948, Czechoslovakia became the victim of a pro-Communist coup d'état instigated by Moscow.

Setting the Plan in Motion

After a long winter of discussion, some stop-gap help, and greatly increased tension in East-West relations, the European Recovery Program was born officially with an act of Congress signed by President Truman in April 1948. To administer the project, a new federal agency, the Economic Cooperation Administration (ECA), was brought into being at the same time, headed by the CEO of the Studebaker automobile company, Paul G. Hoffmann, a Republican, symbolizing bipartisan support for the program. Expenditures began to flow immediately, under tight Congressional supervision.

The program's official enactment identified the supreme objective as creating in Western Europe "a healthy economy independent of extraordinary outside assistance" by 1952. To this end, comments the economic historian Imanuel Wexler, " the act stipulated a recovery plan based on four specific endeavors: (1) a strong production effort, (2) expansion of foreign trade, (3) the creation and maintenance of internal financial stability, and (4) the development of (European) economic cooperation." To the dismay of many Europeans who had counted simply on a big relief program, it soon became clear that such an agenda could only be realized by way of permanent structural change in the European economies, singly and together, as a whole. This was what Marshall had meant when he talked of "a cure rather than a palliative," nothing less.

To meet the challenge, the ongoing Conference on European Economic Cooperation (CEEC) quickly turned itself into the Organization for European Economic Cooperation (OEEC), under the Belgian foreign minister, Paul-Henri Spaak. In the meantime, American embassies in each of the member nations were obtaining signatures on the bilateral pacts which spelled out the obligations of European governments towards their new sponsors. Among them was recognition of the authority of the ECA "Mission" to be set up in each national capital. A formal committee would link each mission to its participating government, in order to supervise the running of the program on the ground.

The committee's key task was to make plans for spending productively the sums in the new "Counterpart Fund." This was a characterizing feature of the whole operation, the tool that most distinguished the Marshall Plan from any conventional aid program. The fund was an account at each national bank specially created to contain the proceeds from the local sale of ERP-supplied goods. Much of the help, it turned out, would not be as free, or as liquid, as the Europeans had imagined. It would instead normally be merchandise sent from the United States and sold to the highest bidder, public or private. Their payments would then go back not to the United States, but into the new fund. From it would come the money to pay for national reconstruction and modernization efforts, as decided between the ECA Mission and the government in each participating capital.

At the same time the ERP was clearly a mighty weapon in the Cold War. Its senior representative in Europe, Ambassador Harriman, went so far in 1949 as to characterize the entire effort as a "fire-fighting operation." Marshall's successor as secretary of state, Dean Acheson, the individual who, in his own words, "probably made as many speeches and answered as many questions about the Marshall Plan as any man alive," remembered that "what citizens and the representatives in Congress always wanted to learn in the last analysis was how Marshall Aid operated to block the extension of Soviet power and the acceptance of Communist economic and political organization and alignment." Against the plan indeed stood the forces of the Cominform, an international propaganda organization set up in October 1947 by the Kremlin with the explicit purpose of combating the Marshall Plan, internationally and—using local Communist parties—within each participating nation. At a time when Communist forces were leading armed insurgency in Greece, looked capable of taking power politically in Italy, seemed to threaten chaos in France, and knew what they wanted in Germany—unlike the West at this stage—the Cold War gave an urgency to the program which concentrated minds everywhere.

Selling the Plan to Its Beneficiaries

From the very beginning the ECA planners had been aware that to tackle the political obstacles their efforts were likely to encounter, they would have to go over the heads of the local governing classes and speak directly to the people. Improvising swiftly, the teams of journalists and filmmakers who launched the ERP "Information Program" turned it, by the end of 1949, into the largest propaganda operation directed by one country to a group of others ever seen in peacetime.

A January 1950 report by Mike Berding, the ERP information director in Rome, instructed:

Carry the message of the Marshall Plan to the people. Carry it to them directly—it won't permeate down. And give it to them so that they can understand it.

No idea seemed too large or daring for the Information Program in its heyday. Workers, managers, and employers were told of the benefits of greater production and productivity, scientific management, and a single-market Europe. In each country there were specialized publications on these subjects, joint committees, trips by European leaders to inspect American factories, conferences and eventually, in some places, even "productivity villages" where model factories and workers' communities could be seen in action. For other groups in society—state employees, teachers, families, even schoolchildren—the promises of the American information campaign were more jobs, higher living standards, and ultimately peace in a Europe without rivalries. The Information Program eventually produced tens of documentary films, hundreds of radio programs, thousands of copies of its pamphlets, and attracted millions of spectators for its mobile exhibitions.

Here posters, models, illuminated displays, audio messages, and films would present the plan as graphically as possible, for every level of understanding. A booklet from a display at the Venice exhibit of summer 1949 opens with a dramatic quantification of the aid arriving at that time: three ships a day, $1,000 a minute, two weeks' salary from every American worker. The goals and the methods of the program are explained in everyday language, with the details explaining how work has been restored to lifeless industries, how new machinery has modernized factories and how greater output is needed Europe-wide to stabilize economic life on a continental scale. The concluding message states that:

> ERP is a unique chance offered to European nations towards reconstructing their economies, raising the standard of living among the masses, and attaining by the year 1952 an economic stability which is the foundation of political independence. ... Every worker, every citizen is bound up in this rebirth. The future and the peace of Italy and of Europe, the general well being of all, depend on the will and the work of each single one of us.

The Plan Evolves

The plan's early years, from June 1948 to the start of the Korean war in June 1950, were remembered by all concerned as the golden epoch of pure economic action and rewards. Experts pointed to the rise of nearly a quarter in the total output of goods and services that the ERP countries enjoyed between 1947 and 1949. They asserted that the "over-all index of production, based on 1938, rose to 115 in 1949, as compared with 77 in 1946 and 87 in 1947." Agriculture, too, recovered, and progress on the inflation front was considered "uneven but definitely encouraging." The foreign trade of the member states was back to its prewar levels, but its most remarkable feature was a change in direction. No longer oriented towards the old European empires, trade was increasing most rapidly within Western Europe, among the ERP members themselves. Experience would show that this was a long-term structural shift in the continent's economy, which within a few years would set going political demands for European integration.

Meanwhile, by the end of 1949 it had become clear that the partner nations had visions of the European Recovery Program that differed in significant respects from those of the American planners when the hard choices came to be made. Across Western Europe, governments badly needed the ERP dollars, but at the same time they sought to make their own deal with what the Americans were offering and, especially, with what they were demanding in exchange. If dependence on the United States there was to be for a while, then it should in any case be conditional, on "our" terms, the Europeans felt.

The British went to extraordinary lengths to resist the Marshall Plan's insistence on immediate economic integration with the rest of Europe, the great string attached to Marshall aid everywhere. The Dutch resisted pressure to start dismantling their empire in the name of free trade. The Austrians refused point blank to reform their railways and their banking system as the Americans desired. The Greek people rejected a new ERP-sponsored currency because they believed that gold sovereigns were the only truly reliable form of monetary exchange. The head of the Italian industrialists told the mission chief in Rome that no matter how cheap synthetic fibers became, Italian women would always prefer clothes made in the home with natural materials. Tinned food might be sold very cheaply, he said, but Italian traditions of cooking would always be preferred. Small firms and traditional artisan skills would be central to Italy's future, just as they had been in the past.

By the start of 1950, practical experience and extensive opinion polling had brought a significant shift in outlook, to the point where the strategists felt obliged to concede that "the majority of Europeans today" had one overriding concern of their own: security. Gradually, in spite of America's reliance on a liberal capitalist economy, the Marshall planners were obliged to recognize the depth of the European commitment to the idea of the non-Communist social welfare state. They insisted simply that its benefits be distributed as widely as possible, to cut the ground from under Communist attacks, both on the plan and on reformist social democratic ideals.

The Impact of Korea

But the unexpected and fear-inspiring turn of events in Asia in 1950 soon put the very existence of the Marshall Plan in doubt. The sharply intensified Cold War confrontation that started with the North Korean invasion of the South in June shortened the project in time and radically transformed it, opening the way to the era of general rearmament and "Mutual Security." Congressional amendments of 1951 and 1952 to the original ERP Act provided $400 million more for a continuing drive to persuade European employers and workers to "accept the American definition of the social and economic desirabilities [sic] of productivity," but now so that military output for national defense against the Soviet threat could be increased at the same time as consumer goods. Everyone was expected to do more for the general effort (hence strengthening NATO), and so rebuild their armed forces, greatly run down since the end of WWII. The ECA men on the ground quickly decided that there was no conflict between America's demand for general rearmament and the traditional ERP objectives: It was just a matter of bending the existing policy goals to the new requirements.

In such a context the successful ERP Information Program soon accelerated into something resembling "psychological warfare," with the world of industry and organized labor identified as the key front in the ideological Cold War against Communism. As one of the ERP's most influential brains, Assistant Administrator (and later Acting Administrator) Richard M. Bissell, explained in Foreign Affairs in April 1951, the United States could wage this war in Europe most effectively by the force of its economic example and the powerful appeal of its consumerist economy to Europeans of all regions and social classes:

> Coca-Cola and Hollywood movies may be regarded as two products of a shallow and crude civilization. But American machinery, American labor relations, and American management and engineering are everywhere respected. ...What is needed is a peaceful revolution which can incorporate into the European economic system certain established and attractive features of our own, ranging from high volumes to collective bargaining. ...[This] will require a profound shift in social attitudes, attuning them to the mid-twentieth century.

The Balance Sheet

In the end, every participating nation succeeded in carrying out its own distinctive version of Richard Bissell's peaceful revolution. Economically, the Marshall Plan mattered far more in Greece, France, Austria, and Holland than it did in Ireland, Norway, or Belgium. For some nations, such as Italy, it was perhaps truly decisive for one year only, for others, the benefits flowed for several years. Each nation made different use of the economic impetus provided by the plan. The Danes secured raw materials and energy supplies. Other peoples, such as those in the German occupation zones, appreciated most the food provided by the ERP. In Italy and

Greece, help with rebuilding railways, roads, and power supplies gave the most lasting benefit. In France, industrial investment came first; in Britain, the Counterpart Fund was almost entirely used to pay wartime debts and re-float sterling.

Both Austria and Sweden, each in its own way, believe that their successful anchorage in the West dates back to the Marshall Plan. If Communist parties grew in Italy and France, they at least did not take control, and these nations remained oriented towards the West. Perhaps Germany was the nation that benefited most overall, as the dynamic of European integration conceived and fostered by the ERP allowed the new Federal Republic to grow in strength and respectability while calming the suspicions of its neighbors. The hoped-for revolution in Franco-German relations did indeed come about. Whatever its other origins in short-term, Cold War necessities, no political development heightened the contrast with the post-World War I era more than this one.

Fifty years after the great experience, Jim Warren, a Marshall planner in Greece, rejoiced:

We had a goal; we had fire in our bellies; we worked like hell; we had tough, disciplined thinking, and we could program, strive for, and see results.

For a short, intense period, a new American presence arrived in Europe, dedicated to finding ways to translate the successes of the American economic experience into recipes for the political salvation of others, and so turn American myth into model. Appreciative

129

Europeans of the time spoke of "a sense of hope and confidence" these American planners brought—of "restored courage and reawakened energy" in the Old World.

In Europe the clash of imported and native models provided the energy to set the great 1950s boom going. The European Recovery Program had supplied the spark to set the chain reaction in motion. In 1957 came the Treaty of Rome, which launched the European Economic Community. Although this scheme of fledgling economic integration was far less radical than the American visionaries of 1949 had demanded, of the inheritance left by the Marshall Plan and its promises, none was more concrete. This founding document initiated Europe's peaceful economic integration, a process that continues to this day.

As for the Americans, following a wobbly emergence in World War I as an international power, they had finally developed foreign policies and a grand strategy "consonant with our new responsibilities as the greatest creditor, greatest producer, and greatest consumer of the 20th century"—as Vera Micheles Dean put it in 1950 in a book entitled Europe and the United States. They had also endowed themselves with a new national image of America as a power that could successfully blend military, political, and economic leadership on an international scale, an image destined to reappear whenever nations turned from war and misery to reach forward towards a new, more hopeful future.

David Ellwood is an associate professor in international history, University of Bologna, and an adjunct professor with Johns Hopkins University's School of Advanced International Studies (SAIS), Bologna Center. His publications on postwar European history include: Italy 1943-1945: The Politics of Liberation *and* Rebuilding Europe: Western Europe, America and Postwar Reconstruction. *His latest project is* America and the Politics of Modernization in Europe, *to be published by Oxford University Press. Professor Ellwood is a 2006 fellow of the Rothermere America Institute at Oxford University.*

9

Brown v. Board of Education: The Law, the Legacy

When the negro writer Ralph Ellison learned of the Supreme Court's *Brown v. Board of Education* decision in May 1954, he exclaimed to a friend, "What a wonderful world of possibilities are unfolded for the children!"

Other negro leaders of the time were equally excited by the Court's unanimous ruling, which struck down state-sponsored racial segregation in the public schools of the United States. Harlem's *Amsterdam News*, a black-owned paper, called the decision the "greatest victory for the negro people since the Emancipation Proclamation." Thurgood Marshall, chief layer for the plaintiffs in the case, recalled, "I was so happy I was numb." Marshall expected state-sponsored school segregation to be wiped out, nationwide, within five years.

❖ ❖ ❖

The enthusiastic expectations of Negro leaders in 1954—and of liberal whites—were entirely understandable. *Brown* (as the decision came to be called) negated a key Supreme Court ruling, *Plessy v. Ferguson* (1896), which had authorized public officials to establish racial segregation so long as separate facilities for blacks and whites were equal. This earlier court decision had sanctioned the doctrine of "separate but equal" in the management of relations between blacks and whites in many areas of the nation.

President Abraham Lincoln had freed American slaves with the Emancipation Proclamation in 1863, during the Civil War. Yet this document hardly led to equality between whites and blacks in America. By 1910, statutory racial segregation was ubiquitous in the 11 states of the American South and widespread in nearby border states (states lying between the North and the South). It affected not only public schools but also hospitals and homes for the elderly, indigent, deaf, and blind. Black people in these states had to use separate rest rooms, drinking fountains, lunch counters, waiting rooms, and railroad cars, and to move to the back of buses and streetcars. Cleverly designed laws barred Negroes from voting in most of these areas.

A host of for-whites-only public accommodations— hotels and motels, restaurants and lunch counters, parks and beaches, swimming pools, libraries, concert halls, and movie theaters—further separated the races. Negro travelers on southern highways never knew where they might find a bed for the night—or even a bathroom. Some recreational areas posted signs, "Negroes [the word then used to identify African Americans] and Dogs Not Allowed."

This rigidly enforced system afflicted public education at every level. All white state universities in the South—and many in the border states—barred African Americans. In 1954, 21 states either mandated or permitted segregation in the public schools. A total of 11.5 million white and black students in 11,173 school districts then attended these schools. They were nearly 39 per cent of America's 28,836,000 public school pupils.

In spite of the *Plessy* decision's requirement for equal facilities, by the early decades of the 20th century it was clear that "separate" by no means meant "equal." Many school buildings for Negroes, especially in the Deep South, were ramshackle wooden structures that lacked heat, electricity, indoor toilet facilities, and running water. Negro pupils, crammed into overcrowded classrooms, shared hand-me-down textbooks no longer needed in the white schools. Their Negro teachers were poorly trained and badly paid. Negro schools commonly lacked cafeterias, auditoriums, libraries, science equipment, and sports programs. Among the plaintiffs in the *Brown* case were pupils from Clarendon County, South Carolina, who had to walk 10 miles round-trip to school because local officials refused to provide bus transportation. Many Negro children in the South, leaving school after the sixth or seventh grades, were scarcely literate.

The *Brown* decision, affirming American ideals of equality and justice, promised to abolish these evils. Desegregation of public schools, enthusiasts like Marshall believed, would not only promote equality of opportunity in education; it would also advance interracial toleration. In time, the races might become integrated in a world wherein skin color would no longer cripple one's chances in life.

What Led to the Brown Decision

The *Brown* decision arose from the efforts of two groups of activists. The first were black parents and liberal white allies who resolved to fight discrimination. Among the earliest of these activists were parents in Clarendon County, South Carolina, who in 1947 demanded provision of school buses for their children. Parents in four other segregated districts—in the states of Virginia, Delaware, and Kansas, and in the District of Columbia—also sought legal assistance. The *Brown* case, combining these five protests into one, took its name from Oliver Brown, a welder and World War II veteran whose daughter, Linda, was barred from attending a white elementary school close to her home in Topeka, Kansas. Instead, she had to arise early, walk across dangerous railroad switching yards, and cross Topeka's busiest commercial street in order to board a bus to take her to an all-Negro school.

At first, Negro parents did not dare to challenge segregation. Instead, they demanded real equality within the "separate but equal" system. In doing so, they aroused fierce local resistance. Whites fired black plaintiffs from their jobs and cut off their credit at local banks. In Clarendon County, hostile whites later burned one of the churches of the Rev. Joseph DeLaine, a Negro protest leader. When white opponents fired at his home in the night, he shot back, jumped into a car, and fled. South Carolina authorities branded him as a fugitive from justice, and he dared not return to his home state.

The second group of activists consisted of lawyers—most of them Negroes—who worked for the Legal Defense Fund (LDF), an autonomous arm of the National Association for the Advancement of Colored People (NAACP). Chief among them was Marshall, a star graduate of Howard University Law School, a predominantly black school in Washington, D.C., that trained many bright attorneys in the 1930s and 1940s. Marshall, a folksy and courageous advocate, had long been managing cases on behalf of Negro causes, notably the desegregation of law schools. Responding to pleas from black parents in Clarendon County, he engaged the LDF in the struggle to promote racial equality in public school systems. In 1950, deciding that true equality could never exist within a separate but equal system, he and other NAACP leaders decided to call for the abolition of racial segregation in the schools.

In retrospect, the decision to fight school segregation seems to have been obvious and necessary. At the time, however, it was a highly controversial move. Many Negroes had no particular wish to send their children to schools with whites. Other Negroes feared that desegregation—if it ever could be achieved—would lead to the closing down of their schools, which, though starved for resources, were nonetheless important institutions of employment and of solidarity in the South. The decision to challenge segregation head-on, moreover, provoked even greater anger among southern whites. Governor Herman Talmadge of Georgia declared that he would never accept integrated schools. He later exclaimed that desegregation would lead to racial intermarriage and to "mongrelization of the races."

But Marshall and his allies pressed ahead, shepherding all five cases through the lower federal courts between 1950 and 1952. Though they lost most of these cases—judges refused to overrule *Plessy*—they took heart from wider developments at the time that promised to advance better race relations. World War II having been waged as a fight for democracy exposed the evils of racism. American statesmen such as President Harry Truman, leading the West in the Cold War, were acutely aware that racial segregation in the United States, mocking American claims to lead the "Free World," had to be challenged. Moreover, millions of southern Negroes were then moving to the North, where they were a great deal freer to organize and where their votes could affect the outcome of local and national elections.

For these and other reasons, many white Americans in the North in the early 1950s were developing doubts about segregation. As one writer later put it, "There was a current of history, and the Court became part of it." Truman, sensitive to the power of this current, had ordered desegregation of America's armed forces in 1948. His Justice Department supported Marshall's legal briefs when the *Brown* cases first reached the Supreme Court for hearing in December 1952.

The Court, however, was an uncertain quantity. Chief Justice Fred Vinson, who hailed from the border state of Kentucky, was one of at least three of the nine justices on the Court who were believed to oppose desegregation of the schools at the time. Two other justices were apparently undecided. It was clear that the Court was deeply divided on the issue—so much so that advocates of racial justice dared not predict victory.

At this point, luck intervened to help the Legal Defense Fund and its plaintiffs. In September 1953, Vinson died suddenly of a heart attack. Hearing of Vinson's death, Justice Felix Frankfurter, a foe of the chief, reputedly commented to an aide, "This is the first indication I have ever had that there is a God." To replace Vinson, President Dwight Eisenhower appointed California Governor Earl Warren as chief. In doing so, the president, a conservative on racial issues, did not anticipate that Warren would advocate the desegregation of schools. But the new chief justice soon surprised him. A liberal at heart, Warren moved quickly to persuade his colleagues to overturn school segregation.

In part because of Warren's efforts, the doubters on the Court swung behind him. Announcing the *Brown* decision in May 1954, Warren stated that racial segregation led to feelings of inferiority among Negro children and damaged their motivation to learn. His opinion concluded, "In the field of public education the doctrine of 'separate but equal' has no place. Separate educational facilities are inherently unequal." Negro children, he argued, had been deprived of the "equal protection" of the laws guaranteed by the 14th Amendment to the United States Constitution.

Putting the Court's Ruling into Practice

This was an historic decision. More than 50 years later, it remains one of the most significant Supreme Court rulings in U.S. history. In focusing on public schools, *Brown* aimed at the core of segregation. It subsequently served as a precedent for Court decisions in the late 1950s that ordered the desegregation of other public facilities—beaches, municipal golf courses, and (following a year-long black boycott in 1955-56) buses in Montgomery, Alabama. It was obvious, moreover, that no other governmental institution in the early 1950s— not the presidency under Eisenhower, not the Congress (which was dominated by southerners)—was prepared to attack racial segregation. It was no wonder that Ellison, Marshall, and many others hailed the ruling as a pivotal moment in American race relations.

It soon became obvious, however, that *Brown* would not work wonders. Like many Supreme Court decisions in American history, the ruling was limited to specific issues raised by the cases. Thus, it did not explicitly concern itself with many other forms of racial segregation—as in public accommodations—or with more informal but pervasive forms of racial discrimination, as in voting and employment. It deliberately avoided challenging a host of state laws that outlawed racial intermarriage. Targeting only publicly sponsored school segregation, *Brown* had no direct legal impact on schools in other parts of the nation. There, racially imbalanced schools were less the result of state or local laws (of *de jure* discrimination) than of informal actions (*de facto* discrimination) based on the reality of races inhabiting different neighborhoods. In the 1950s, as later, *de facto* segregated neighborhoods—and schools—flourished in the American North.

The *Brown* decision was cautious in another way: because Warren and his fellow justices feared to push segregating districts too hard, they did not order the immediate dismantling of school segregation. Instead, they deliberated for a year, at which point they issued a second ruling, *Brown II*, which avoided specifying what sort of racial balance might constitute compliance. Refusing to set a specific deadline for action, *Brown II* stated that desegregation should be carried out with "all deliberate speed." This fuzzy phrase encouraged southern white authorities to procrastinate and gave federal courts in the South little guidance in resolving disputes that were already arising.

It is virtually certain, however, that whatever the Court might have said in 1954-55, and no matter how slowly it was willing to go, southern whites would have fought fiercely against enforcement of *Brown*. Indeed, and most ironically, schools then and later proved the most sensitive and resistant of America's public institutions to changes in racial relations. Though many districts in the border states slowly desegregated, whites in the Deep South (often aided by the Ku Klux Klan and other extremist groups) bitterly opposed change. In 1956, virtually all southerners in Congress issued the so-called Southern Manifesto pledging to oppose school desegregation by "all lawful means." In 1957, Arkansas Governor Orval Faubus openly defied the Court, forcing a reluctant President Eisenhower—who never endorsed the *Brown* decision—to send in federal troops to enforce token desegregation of Central High School in Little Rock. There—as in New Orleans, Nashville, Charlotte, and many other places—angry whites took to the streets in order to harass and intimidate black pupils on their way to school. In 1964, 10 years after *Brown*, fewer than 2 percent of black students in the South attended public schools with whites.

Impetus for the Civil Rights Movement

Thereafter, liberals finally made progress in their fight for the desegregation of schools. The driving force behind their gains was the civil rights movement, which swelled with enormous speed and power between 1960 and 1965. In 1964-65, pressure from the movement compelled Congress to approve two historic laws, the Civil Rights Act of 1964 and the Voting Rights Act of 1965. Vigorously enforced by federal officials within the administration of President Lyndon Johnson (1963-69), these measures succeeded in virtually demolishing a host of discriminatory racial practices, including segregation in public accommodations. In particular, the Civil Rights Act authorized cutting off federal financial aid to local school districts that continued to evade the message of *Brown*. Responding to the more militantly liberal temper of the times, the federal courts, including the Supreme Court, began ordering school officials not only to desegregate without delay but also to establish "racial balance." By the late 1970s, roughly 40 percent of black public school pupils in the South were attending schools in which the student population was at least 50 percent white.

What did the *Brown* decision have to do with the rise of the civil rights movement—and therefore with these dramatic changes? In considering this question, scholars and others have offered varied answers. When the movement shot forward in the early 1960s, many
142

people believed that *Brown* was a crucial catalyst of it. Then and later they have also argued that this first major decision energized and emboldened what became known as the liberal "Warren Court," which zealously advanced the rights of minorities, criminal defendants, poor people, and others in need of legal protection. Among the men who helped to propel this liberal judicial surge was Thurgood Marshall, whom Johnson named as America's first black Supreme Court justice in 1967.

Today, most scholars agree that *Brown* was symbolically useful to leaders of the civil rights movement. After all, the law, at last, was on their side. "Separate but equal" no longer enjoyed constitutional sanction. They also agree that *Brown*, the first key decision of the Warren Court, stimulated a broader rights consciousness that excited and in many ways empowered other groups—women, the elderly, the disabled, gay people, and other minorities—after 1960. These are the most important long-range legacies of the decision.

It is not so clear, however, that *Brown* was uniformly effective in the task it was supposed to accomplish, which was to promote complete desegregation of public school systems. On the contrary, by 1960 it was apparent that the legal strategies employed by men such as Marshall had failed to achieve desegregation of the schools. Realizing the limitations of litigation, which moved slowly, civil rights leaders like the Reverend Martin Luther King Jr., as well as militant activists in organizations like the Congress of Racial Equality (CORE) and the Student Nonviolent Coordinating Committee (SNCC), seized on strategies of direct action. One strategy was "sit-ins," where crowds of blacks sat down in places they weren't supposed to go in the segregated South. Another was "freedom rides," where activists boarded buses headed South to force desegregation of national bus lines and bus terminals—actions that provoked violent responses by mobs of local whites. There were also mass demonstrations. These confrontations, unleashing violence that flashed across millions of TV screens, shocked Americans into demanding that the government take action to protect the ideals and values of the nation.

The Brown Decision Today

Since the 1950s, America's race relations have greatly improved. White attitudes are more liberal. A considerable black middle class has arisen. Some "affirmative action" policies aimed at preventing discrimination, scarcely imagined in the 1950s and 1960s, have secured Supreme Court approval. The historic civil rights laws of the 1960s continue to enjoy solid political support. Talented African Americans have risen to a range of leadership positions, including secretary of state of the United States. Thanks in part to the change in society and culture signaled and indeed initiated by *Brown*, the Bad Old Days of constitutionally sanctioned, state-sponsored segregation are gone forever.

But it is also obvious that *Brown* has not changed everything. In the 2000s, considerable racial inequality persists in the United States. The median income of blacks, though far better in real terms than earlier, remains at around 70 percent of median white income. Millions of African Americans continue to reside in central city areas where poverty, crime, and drug addiction remain serious. Though *de jure* segregation is, of course, now banned, barriers of income, culture, and mutual distrust still often separate the races. Especially in urban areas, public schools have re-segregated since the mid-1980s. In the '70s and '80s, courts, seeking to create racially balanced schools, mandated a certain amount of complex busing of pupils from one school district to another, at the local level. Labeled "forced busing" by its opponents, this action proved wildly unpopular among many whites. Thus, while many liberals have opposed re-segregation in recent years, they have received relatively little support from the courts, which since the 1990s have generally ruled that *de facto* residential segregation, not intentionally racist public policies, have promoted this re-segregating process, and that such segregation is not subject to further attempts at judicial reversal. Many black people, concerned, like whites, above all with sending their children to good schools, have concluded that engaging in protracted legal battles for educational desegregation plans involving busing or other complicated methods is no longer worth the effort or the expense.

Today, the percentage of black students in the South that attend white majority public schools has declined to around 30. Because many northern industrial cities by now have overwhelmingly black populations in parts of their central cores, the percentages of black students attending such schools outside the South are even lower. Hispanic Americans also often attend racially imbalanced schools. Many schools mainly attended by minority students are inferior—in per pupil spending and the training of teachers, certainly in levels of student achievement—to predominantly white schools in nearby affluent suburban districts.

If Ralph Ellison or Thurgood Marshall were alive today, each would undoubtedly be pleased that *Brown* ultimately helped to kill *de jure* school segregation. But they would also recognize that the dramatic decision, while a necessary step toward the promotion of racial justice, did not lead to the establishment of a uniformly integrated society. Whites and blacks in the United States are far more integrated than they were 50 years ago, especially in the workplace. But in the United States, as elsewhere in the world, the struggle to create societies where all are truly equal has yet to achieve its goal.

James T. Patterson, an historian of modern America, retired from teaching at Brown University in 2002. His recent books include Grand Expectations: The United States, 1945-1974 *(winner of the Bancroft Prize in history);* Brown v. Board of Education: A Civil Rights Milestone and Its Troubled Legacy; *and* Restless Giant: The United States from Watergate to *Bush v. Gore.*

10

The Right to Legal Counsel: The Gideon v. Wainwright Decision

Until Clarence Earl Gideon mailed his envelope to the United States Supreme Court, there was nothing about him to suggest that he would become a celebrated symbol of fairness in American justice. As the year 1962 began, Gideon sat in a Florida prison, scribbling an appeal to the Supreme Court. He had been given a five-year prison sentence for the crime of breaking and entering into a poolroom in Panama City, Florida. (In the United States, most criminal matters fall under state jurisdiction.) By all appearances, he was one of life's chronic losers, a boozy 51-year-old semi-educated petty criminal who had spent a substantial portion of his life behind bars.

But Gideon was the beneficiary of two factors that were destined to transform him into an iconic figure in American law. First, he had a passionate belief that his conviction was unconstitutional because he had been tried without a lawyer. Second, the tide of constitutional history in the United States was on his side.

❖ ❖ ❖

When Gideon had been brought to trial he insisted that he, a poor man, was constitutionally entitled to have a lawyer appointed to defend his case. The trial judge explained that under Florida law only defendants in capital cases (cases that could result in the death penalty) were entitled to have lawyers appointed to defend them.

Gideon stubbornly insisted: "The United States Supreme Court says I am entitled to be represented by counsel."

The Judge said no and ordered Gideon to represent himself. Gideon did so, badly, and was convicted and sentenced to the maximum, five years.

So when Clarence Gideon later mailed his handwritten appeal to the U. S. Supreme Court, he had created an unambiguous record that he had demanded his right to be represented by a lawyer, and his demand had been denied. His problem was, he was wrong—the Supreme Court had never ruled that a defendant in a state trial always has a right to be represented by a lawyer. But what Clarence Earl Gideon could never have imagined was that powerful forces were in play that

149

would eventually persuade the Supreme Court to see things Gideon's way.

Extending the Bill of Rights to State Courts

Americans' constitutional rights are so vigorously enforced these days that it is easy to forget that until the second half of the 20th century, the Bill of Rights was virtually ignored in the nation's state courts, where most crimes were prosecuted. The reason was that the framers of the first 10 amendments to the Constitution, known as the Bill of Rights, had made a mistaken assumption as to where the greatest threat to their liberties lay. These 18th-century Americans had assumed that, if a tyrannical government were to threaten their rights, it would be the newly created federal government, running roughshod over the rights of the people of the states. They felt that the state governments, so close to the people, would never abuse the citizens so close at hand.

Thus the Bill of Rights contained no language protecting the peoples' rights against abusive state and local officials. The First Amendment began: "Congress shall pass no law..." and then it and the other amendments to the U.S. Constitution proceeded to list the rights that the federal government must respect. The list began with free speech, free press, and freedom of religion, included a ban on unreasonable searches by police, a ban on compelled testimony in court, and other
150

safeguards, and (in the Sixth Amendment) the Bill of Rights guaranteed each person accused of a federal crime "the assistance of counsel for his defense." So Clarence Earl Gideon did, indeed, have a constitutional right to a lawyer—if he had been tried in federal court. Fortunately for him, a feeling had been growing in the United States that these same constitutional rights should be binding on the states.

When the framers of the Bill of Rights assumed that the states would not mistreat the citizens close at hand, they were only half wrong. Most average citizens were treated fairly by state and local officials. But too often society's underdogs—the poor, the uneducated, non-whites—were not. As the years and decades passed, the feeling grew in the United States, and particularly among some members of the Supreme Court, that the political process in some of the states was failing to protect the rights of all the people—and that if those rights were to be protected, the Supreme Court would have to do it by requiring state and local officials to abide by the Bill of Rights.

But how could the Supreme Court justify this extension, since the Bill of Rights by its terms limited only the federal government? The answer was found in the Fourteenth Amendment to the Constitution, which had been enacted after the Civil War as a way to protect the newly freed slaves from discriminatory southern officials. The Fourteenth Amendment—unlike the Bill of Rights—was specifically aimed at the states. It declared that they could not deprive any person of life, liberty, or property without "due process of law" or deny any person "the equal protection of the laws." These were ambiguous constitutional rights that were difficult to apply to any individual case, but if the due process guarantee in the Fourteenth Amendment could be construed to require the states to obey the specific protections of the Bill of Rights, the result would, experts knew, be a revolutionary expansion of Americans' constitutional rights.

Thus some justices of the Supreme Court began to argue that if any of the guarantees contained in the Bill of Rights could be shown to be fundamental to the concept of a just society, then those provisions of the Bill of Rights would be "absorbed" into the due process guarantee of the Fourteenth Amendment and made enforceable against the states. Was the Sixth Amendment's guarantee of the right to counsel so fundamental and essential to a fair trial that it should be binding on the states in all cases? Clarence Earl Gideon had unknowingly brought this question before the Supreme Court.

Gideon's Appeal and the Civil Rights Movement

When the Supreme Court announced in June of 1962 that it would hear Gideon's case in order to consider if the Sixth Amendment's right to counsel was binding on the states, Gideon's cause faced a daunting handicap. Twenty-one years earlier the Supreme Court had considered that same issue in another case, and had decided against the position urged by Gideon. The Supreme

Court has been known to overturn its own past decisions, but not often. In Gideon's case, the justices could not even demonstrate that conditions had changed since the earlier decision. If the Court was going to rule for Gideon, it would have to swallow the bitter pill of admitting that in its earlier decision it had simply been wrong.

But on a more subtle level, Gideon's cause had much going for it. There was a broad feeling in the country in the 1960s, a high point of modern liberalism, that state and local officials too often ran roughshod over the rights of minorities and the poor, and that the legislatures in the offending states seemed unlikely to do much about it—at least, in the absence of pressure from the Supreme Court. The underlying issue was mistreatment of blacks in southern states in the form of legal segregation, violence, and denial of voting rights. Though enfranchised after the Civil War, they were systematically discriminated against. In the aftermath of World War II, newspapers and the new technology of television brought these grim vestiges of slavery to the attention of the American public as a whole.

The Supreme Court had begun the process of applying pressure on southern states in a string of desegregation decisions. In general, public opinion seemed to favor this liberal activism by the Supreme Court—or at least to tolerate it as a necessary overstepping of traditional judicial bounds. So by the early 1960s the Supreme Court was poised to go forward, in a case-by-case process, to decide which of the Bill of Rights' safeguards were so "fundamental" that they were binding on the states. The result has been called a "due process revolution."

When the Supreme Court announced that it had granted the appeal of an obscure Florida convict to decide if all states must provide lawyers for the accused, Clarence Gideon immediately became the subject of great public interest. There was something romantic about the poorly educated inmate, scribbling with a pencil a legal petition that brought to the Supreme Court a question of basic fairness in American law. Gideon's appeal also put a human face on the abstract debate over American justice. To have brought Gideon without a lawyer to trial for his freedom, pitted against an experienced lawyer for the prosecution, was so stark and dramatic that it struck the average American as unfair.

In a subtle manner, Gideon also came to be associated with the movement for greater civil rights for American blacks. Gideon was a white man. But he had lived his life at the bottom of the social and economic ladder, as many nonwhites had, and he had suffered in court because of his poverty. Many blacks felt that they had been disadvantaged in court (and outside it) for the same reasons, so they felt that Gideon's cause was also theirs. The Supreme Court appointed famed Washington lawyer (and later a justice of the Court) Abe Fortas to represent Gideon in his Supreme Court case. Fortas considered the Supreme Court's refinement of the criminal law and its expansion of civil rights as a related process, part of an overall effort by society to civilize itself. "I believe," he said, "that if you think of the developments in the racial field, you will see a parallel which similarly, in my opinion, indicates that in the past generation, we as a people have been moving forward towards a better, a greater, and a nobler conception of the rights of man, and I think Gideon is part of that movement."

So the stakes were high on March 18, 1963, when the Supreme Court announced its decision in the Gideon case. Without a dissent, the Court ruled that the Sixth Amendment's right to counsel is binding on the states. "In our adversary system of criminal justice," the Court's opinion said, "any person haled into court, who is too poor to hire a lawyer, cannot be assured a fair trial unless counsel is provided for him." The justices overturned Gideon's conviction. Immediately, the nation understood that the decision reached far beyond justice for Gideon. It meant that the Supreme Court had embarked on a process that would strengthen the constitutional protections of rich and poor alike. (Meanwhile, Gideon gained his own measure of justice. He was brought to trial again by the state of Florida, this time represented by a local lawyer appointed by the court. The jury found Gideon not guilty.)

The Debate over the Constitution as "Living Document"

The *Gideon* decision by the Supreme Court raised a series of immediate questions. Among them: How could the states afford to supply lawyers to all indigent defendants? If poor suspects were entitled to lawyers during their interrogations, wouldn't the lawyers tell them to remain silent and undermine the efforts of the police? What would be the impact of setting free all the prisoners who had been convicted without the assistance of lawyers?

But far more important were broader issues that the *Gideon* decision had raised. If the Sixth Amendment's right to counsel was so fundamental that the states had to obey it, clearly the Supreme Court would say other provisions of the Bill of Rights were also binding on the states. Indeed, by the end of the 1960s the Court had issued a series of decisions, requiring the states to obey most of the remaining safeguards of the Bill of Rights. The list of these safeguards imposed upon the states is as follows: the prohibition against unreasonable searches (Fourth Amendment); against "double jeopardy"—that is, being tried again if acquitted the first time—against compelled testimony against oneself (Fifth Amendment); the right of each defendant to a speedy and public trial by an impartial jury, to be confronted with the witnesses against him, and to have compulsory process for obtaining witnesses in his favor

(Sixth Amendment); and the prohibition against cruel and unusual punishments (Eighth Amendment).

Unfortunately for the Supreme Court, these decisions were issued during a time of rapidly growing violent crime and civil unrest in the United States. Critics of the Court blamed this on the justices, and Richard Nixon repeatedly chided the Court in his successful campaign for president in 1968. Other politicians have done so as well. However, presidents influence federal court decisions for the most part through judicial appointments, which may arise infrequently.

In addition, on a theoretical level, the due process revolution had left a lingering question that remains unresolved into the 21st century. The American system of government is based on a written constitution, which is interpreted by the Supreme Court. If the Supreme Court has been faithful in interpreting the Constitution down through the years, how could it suddenly discover, in the mid-20th century, a vast body of new law enhancing the rights of minorities and criminal defendants? As the dean of the Harvard Law School, Erwin N. Griswold, wryly put it in 1965, "Some things have recently been found in the Federal Constitution that were not previously known to be there."

Defenders of the Court argue that the Constitution is a "living document," which would become obsolete if the justices did not interpret it in a way to keep it relevant to the issues of changing times. Their most persuasive case in point has been *Brown v. Board of Education*, the 1954 decision that declared school segregation unconstitutional. To reach that outcome the Court had to overrule a half-century of decisions that said separate but equal facilities for blacks satisfied the Constitution. How, the Court's defenders asked, could the Court not rule in the increasingly tolerant and cosmopolitan mid-20th century, that state-enforced racial segregation violated the Constitution?

But critics of the "living document" approach argue that this is an invitation to activist judges to write their own notions of desirable social policy into the Constitution. The critics often cite, as an example of this, the Supreme Court's decision in *Roe v. Wade*, the 1973 decision that established a constitutional right for women to obtain abortions. The Court's opinion held that laws forbidding abortions violated the privacy rights of women and their physicians to make decisions involving abortions without interference from the state. The critics point out that the Constitution and the Bill of Rights say nothing about privacy rights, and they allege that the justices concocted an implied right of privacy in order to arrive at a result they considered desirable.

This constitutional debate has evolved into a heated political struggle. Liberals, for the most part, favor the "living Constitution" approach, while conservatives argue that judges should leave lawmaking to the legislatures. One result has been an ongoing political dispute over the appointment and confirmation of judges—particularly nominees to sit on the Supreme Court—a dispute that shows no sign of ending.

After his acquittal, Clarence Earl Gideon drifted from one Florida tavern to the next until January 18, 1972, when he died at the age of 61. That same year, the Supreme Court expanded its ruling in his case to require counsel for any defendant who, if convicted, might spend even one day in jail.

Gideon was initially buried in an unmarked grave. Donors later provided a headstone with this inscription: "Each era finds an improvement in law for the benefit of mankind."

Fred Graham has been a legal journalist since becoming Supreme Court correspondent for The New York Times *in 1965. In 1972, he switched media, becoming law correspondent for CBS Television News, and in 1989 was hired by the then-new television legal network, Court TV, to be its chief anchor and managing editor. He is now Court TV's senior editor, stationed in Washington, D.C. Mr. Graham has a law degree from Vanderbilt University and a Diploma in Law as a Fulbright Scholar at Oxford University.*

11

The Immigration Act of 1965: Intended and Unintended Consequences

When Lyndon Johnson signed the Immigration Act of 1965 at the foot of the Statute of Liberty on October 3 of that year, he stressed the law's symbolic importance over all:

> This bill that we will sign today is not a revolutionary bill. It does not affect the lives of millions. It will not re-shape the structure of our daily lives, or really add importantly to either our wealth or our power. Yet it is still one of the most important acts of this Congress and of this Administration [as it] corrects a cruel and enduring wrong in the conduct of the American nation.

The President from Texas was not being uncharacteristically modest. Johnson was saying what his advisor and "experts" had told him.

❖ ❖ ❖

Little noted at the time and ignored by most historians for decades, the 1965 law is now regarded as one of three 1965 statutes that denote the high-water mark of late 20th-century American liberalism. (The other two are the Voting Rights Act, which enforced the right of African Americans to vote, and the Medicare/Medicaid Act, which financed health care for older Americans and for persons in poverty.) The Immigration Act was chiefly responsible for the tremendous surge in immigration in the last third of the 20th century (as Table I on page 80 shows) and also greatly heightened the growing incidence of Latin Americans and Asians in the mix of arrivals to the United States in the decades that followed.

Why did the president's experts so markedly misjudge the myriad potential consequences of the new law? Because they focused on old battles while failing to analyze the actual changes which had already occurred by that date. Indeed, to understand the nature of the changes wrought and who was able to come to America as a result of the new law, it is necessary to examine the prior course of American immigration policy.

American Immigration Policy Before 1921

Prior to 1882, there were no significant restrictions on any group of free immigrants who wanted to settle in the United States of America. In that year, however, Congress passed the somewhat misnamed Chinese Ex-clusion Act (it barred only Chinese laborers) and began a 61-year period of ever more restrictive immigration policies. By 1917, immigration had been limited in sev-en major ways. First, most Asians were barred as a group. Among immigrants as a whole, certain criminals, people who failed to meet certain moral standards, those with various diseases and disabilities, paupers or "persons likely to become a public charge," some radi-cals, and illiterates were specifically barred. Yet, in spite of such restrictions, total immigration—except during the difficult years of World War I—continued to grow throughout the final two decades of the 19th century and the first two of the 20th.

Perhaps because of the influx, anti-immigrant sen-timent among nativists heightened when a sharp post-World War I economic downturn combined with fears about the Bolshevik Revolution of 1917 and left-wing domestic radicalism resulted in a panic about a largely imaginary flood of European immigration. The chair-man of the immigration committee of the House of Rep-resentatives, Albert Johnson, a Republican representing a rural district in Washington state, used excerpts from consular reports to argue that the country was in danger of being swamped by "abnormally twisted" and "unassimilable" Jews, "filthy, un-American and often dangerous in their habits." While those views were extreme for the time, the consensus of Congress was that too many Southern and Eastern Europeans, predominantly Catholics and Jews, were coming into the country—and this view was clearly shared by many if not most Americans in those days. Spurred by such distaste, if not alarm, in the 1920-21 winter session of Congress, the House of Representatives voted 293-46 in favor of a 14-month suspension of all immigration.

The somewhat less alarmist Senate rejected the notion of zero immigration and substituted a bill sponsored by Senator William P. Dillingham, a Vermont Republican. His plan was agreed to by Congress but was vetoed by the outgoing president, Woodrow Wilson. The new Congress repassed it without record vote in the House and 78-1 in the Senate. Wilson's successor, President Warren G. Harding, signed it in May 1921.

Immigration Quotas of the 1920s

The 1921 act was a benchmark law placing the first numerical limits, called quotas, on most immigration. A similar but more drastic version—the version that Lyndon Johnson complained about—was enacted in 1924. Then and later attention focused on the quotas, but they did not apply to all immigrants. Two kinds of immigrants could be admitted "without numerical limitation": wives—but not husbands—and unmarried children under 18 of U.S. citizens, and immigrants from Western Hemisphere nations.

Nations outside the Western Hemisphere were assigned quotas based originally on the percentage of the population from that nation among the foreign-born as recorded in the census of 1890, which restrictionists called the Anglo-Saxon census because it preceded the large influx of Southern and Eastern Europeans. (After 1929 an allegedly scientific method was used to reduce immigration even further.) Under both regimens, nations of Northwest Europe got the lion's share of new slots for immigrants, even though already for decades most immigrants had come from Eastern and Southern Europe.

The 1924 law also barred "aliens ineligible to citizenship"—reflecting the fact that American law had, since 1870, permitted only "white persons" and those "of African descent" to become naturalized citizens. The purpose of this specific clause was to keep out Japanese, as other Asians had been barred already. (American law at the time defined Asians in terms of degrees of latitude and longitude, a provision that left only those living west of Afghanistan eligible for immigration to the United States.) And, as a further control, all immigrants, quota and non-quota, were required to obtain entry visas into the United States from U.S. consuls in their country of origin before leaving. While some American foreign service officers were "immigrant friendly," many, perhaps most, refused visas to persons who were legally eligible for admission. The State Department's instructions to its consular officials emphasized rejection rather than admission. A 1930 directive, for example, provided that:

If the consular officer believes that the applicant may probably be a public charge at any time, even during a considerable period subsequent to his arrival, he must refuse the visa.

But even with the new restrictions, significant numbers of immigrants continued to be admitted throughout the 1920s. In fact, the 1929 figure—almost 280,000 new immigrants—would not be reached again until 1956. The Great Depression and World War II reduced immigration drastically. As Table 2 on page 81 shows, both the number and incidence of foreign-born in the nation fell. In each census from 1860 to 1920 the census recorded that about one American in seven was foreign-born; by 1970 that figure had dropped to fewer than one in 20.

Americans came to believe that the era of immigration was over. The leading historian of American nativism, John Higham, would write in his 1955 classic, *Strangers in the Land*, that:

Although immigration of some sort would continue, the vast folk movements that had formed one of the most fundamental social forces in American history had been brought to an end. The old belief in America as a promised land for all who yearn for freedom had lost its operative significance.

Although no one seems to have perceived it, the era of ever increasing immigration restriction had come to an end a dozen years before.

Refugees and Other Wartime Changes

In December 1943, at the urging of President Franklin D. Roosevelt, who wished to make a gesture of support to a wartime ally, Congress repealed the 15 statutes excluding immigrants from China, gave a minimal immigration quota to Chinese, and, most important of all, made Chinese aliens eligible for naturalization. Three years later Congress passed similar laws giving the same rights to Filipinos and "natives of India," and in 1952 it erased all racial or ethnic bars to the acquisition of American citizenship. Unlike immigration legislation of the pre-World War II era, these and many subsequent changes in laws were motivated by foreign policy concerns rather than concern about an anti-immigrant backlash among domestic constituents.

In addition, before 1952 other changes had taken place as well in American policy. It had begun to make special provision for refugees. In the run-up to World War II, Congress had refused to make such provision, most notably by blocking a vote on a bill admitting 20,000 German children, almost all of whom would have been Jewish. Former President Herbert Hoover backed it; President Roosevelt privately indicated that he favored it but in the end refused to risk his prestige

166

by supporting it. Historians and policy makers would come, in the wake of the Holocaust, to condemn American failure to provide a significant haven for refugees from Hitler, though in point of fact many Jewish refugees did make it on their own to American shores. Vice President Walter Mondale spoke for a consensus in 1979 when he judged that the United States and other nations of asylum had at least in this sense "failed the test of civilization" before and during World War II by not being more unreservedly generous to Hitler's potential victims.

Thus, the first of three bitter post-World War II legislative battles over immigration policy was fought between 1946 and 1950 and focused on refugees. By the end of 1946, some 90 percent of the perhaps 10 million refugees in Europe had been resettled largely in their former homelands. The remainder, referred to as displaced persons, or DPs, were people who literally had no place to go. Although DPs were often perceived as a "Jewish problem," only about a fifth of the 1.1 million remaining DPs were Jews. Many of these wished to go to Palestine, then mandated to Britain, which refused to allow them to enter.

President Harry S Truman tried for nearly two years to solve the problem by executive action because Congress and most Americans were opposed to any increase in immigration in general, and to Jewish immigration in particular. At the beginning of 1947 he asked Congress to find ways in which the United States could fulfill its "responsibilities to these homeless and suffering refugees of all faiths." This is the first presidential suggestion that the nation had a "responsibility" to accept refugees. It has been echoed by each president since then.

Truman himself sent no program to Congress. We now know, as many suspected then, that the White House worked closely with a citizens committee which soon announced a goal of 400,000 refugee admissions. Success came in two increments. In June 1948, Congress passed a bill admitting 202,000 DPs, but with restrictions that many refugee advocates felt discriminated against Jews and Catholics. Truman signed it reluctantly, knowing that was the best he was going to get from Congress at that point. Two years later he signed a second bill which increased the total to 415,000 and dropped the provisions that he had complained about.

To create the illusion for their edgy constituents that the traditional quota system was still intact, Congress pretended that the immigrants admitted by these bills above their national quotas represented, in essence, "mortgages" that would be "paid off" by reducing quotas for those nations in future years. This manifestly could not be done. To cite an extreme example, the annual Latvian quota of 286 was soon "mortgaged" until the year 2274! Congress quietly cancelled all such "mortgages" in 1957.

In the event some 410,000 DPs were actually admitted. Only about one in six were Jews; almost as many, about one in seven, were Christian Germans expelled from Czechoslovakia and other Eastern European nations. Most of the rest were Stalin's victims, persons who had been displaced by the Soviet takeover of Eastern Europe, mainly Poles and persons from the Baltic Republics.

Continuing Controversy over the Quota System

While the immediate postwar refugee battle ended in favor of admitting at least some refugees, the bitterness about immigration continued in an ongoing debate about revising the basic statutes largely unchanged since 1924. The resulting statute, the 1952 Immigration and Nationality Act (INA), also known as the McCarran-Walter Act, was passed over Truman's veto while the Korean War raged. President Truman and most other liberals (but, interestingly, not Senator—later President—Lyndon Johnson) were repelled by a kind of side issue: the act's Cold War aspects which applied a strict ideological litmus test not only to immigrants but also to visitors. Under the provisions of the act, many European intellectuals, such as Jean Paul Sartre, could not lecture at American universities.

Truman's veto message (overridden in the end by Congress), praised the act's abolition of all purely racial and ethnic bars to naturalization per se, its expansion of family reunification, and elimination of gender discrimination. But the president said the INA "would continue, practically without change, the national origins quota system." President Truman and most subsequent commentators really failed to understand the full potential impact of the limited changes wrought by the McCarran Act. In particular, they neglected to consider the potential effect of those wrought by an obscure provision— Section 212(d)(5)—which gave any future president discretionary parole power to admit unlimited numbers of aliens "for emergency reasons or...in the public interest." In practice this meant that later presidents would order, for example, the admission of large numbers of Hungarian, Cuban, Tibetan, or Southeast Asian refugees and Congress would later regularize that action.

Analysis of all admissions during the 13 years that the INA was in effect (1953-65) shows that some 3.5 million immigrants legally entered the U.S. Just over a third were quota immigrants. Non-quota immigrants were an absolute majority in every single year. Asian immigrants, supposedly limited under an "Asia-Pacific triangle" clause to 2,000 per annum, actually numbered 236,000, almost 10 times the prescribed amount. Family members of native-born or newly naturalized Asian Americans accounted for most of these. In addition, the INA years mark the first period in American history in which European immigrants did not dominate free immigration: 48 percent were from Canada, the Caribbean, and Latin America, with the largest number from Mexico. Seven percent were from Asia, and only 43 percent from Europe.

The 1965 Immigration Act

Although the national origins system was no longer dominant, in the 1960s its last-ditch defense was led in the Senate by Sam J. Ervin, a North Carolina Democrat, who later, in the 1970s, was to become a hero to liberals for his role in the Watergate hearings. But, in 1965, Ervin took a conservative stance, arguing that the existing quota system, as modified, was not discriminatory but was rather "like a mirror reflecting the United States." What Ervin and others who supported similar "cultural" arguments for restriction never admitted was that their "mirrors" were distorted, reflecting not the United States as it was already becoming in 1965, but as it was profiled decades earlier in the 1920 census. Their cause was doomed as many Americans adopted more cosmopolitan views.

In any event, spurred in part by the liberal ideological climate of the 1960s, the new law once and for all abolished national quotas and substituted hemispheric caps: 170,000 for the Eastern Hemisphere, and 120,000 for the Western, with a limit of 20,000 annually from any nation. These caps seemed to set an annual limit of 290,000 on immigration, but that was an illusion. As had been true of its predecessors since 1921, there were provisions for immigrants whose entry was authorized outside of numerical limits. The new law expanded the categories of family members who could enter without numerical limit, and reserved most of the enumerated slots for more distant family members of citizens and even some family members of resident aliens.

There was a seeming cap on refugees. The new law set aside 6 percent of the overall global immigration cap for them (amounting at the time to 17,400 visas annually), but left the McCarran Act's presidential parole power intact. Thus by century's end more than three million refugees had come from Hungary, Cuba, Vietnam, Tibet, and elsewhere, initially admitted by parole and later regularized by Congress.

But the bulk of the 22.8 million immigrants who entered between 1966 and 2000 were family members of recent immigrants participating in continuing streams of so-called "chain migration," with arriving immigrants making still other family members potential future immigrants. Fewer of those immigrants came from Europe. The chart below shows regional shares.

No one in 1965 could have envisioned this result. It is common to attribute the liberalization of immigration requirements to the lessening of racial and ethnic prejudice in America over time, a social trend that has resulted in diversity rather than homogeneity in population as an ideal among many. Most authorities, however, would give even greater weight to the changing goals of American foreign policy. They argue that immigration policy is a subset of foreign policy and that the monocultural goals of policies laid down in the 1920s were inappropriate for a nation seeking global leadership.

An analysis of the kinds of persons who have come to America since 1965 reveals both similarities with and differences from those who came in the classic age of heavy immigration between the end of the Napoleonic Wars and 1924. The major continuity is that most immigrants in both eras came to work, and employers were able to pay them less than the going rate. But other factors are quite different. No longer do most immigrants arrive from Europe. Other differences include gender—earlier immigrants were overwhelmingly male, and since 1950 there has been a slight female majority. And the differences include educational and skill levels. Most earlier immigrants had educational and skill levels below those of the average American, while in recent years a sizeable minority is highly skilled. In fact, it has become common to speak of a "brain drain" from the origin countries. Absolute majorities of contemporary immigrants can be described as coming from developing nations.

When we examine all global migration flows, we find that Europe, which since the Age of Discovery had been an exporter of population, has become in the post-World War II era a target for immigration, often from former colonies. Many Europeans were slow to recognize these changes. When former German Chancellor Helmut Kohl made his claim that Germany had never been a nation of immigrants, the census showed that the Federal Republic had a slightly larger percentage of foreign-born residents than did the United States.

In the current era of globalization, most advanced industrial nations are deeply involved with immigration. In the United States, despite the tightened security measures resulting in part from the horrors of 9/11, immigration flows have continued high. The dual phenomena of importing labor and at the same time exporting jobs—overseas "outsourcing"—while increasing corporate profits and growth of the economy, have also exacerbated social stresses that may well increase, at least in the short term.

Roger Daniels is a professor emeritus of history at the University of Cincinnati. Author of 16 books and editor of some 90, he served as historical consultant to the Presidential Commission on the Relocation and Internment of Civilians and on the committee which helped plan the immigration museum on Ellis Island. Recent books are: Coming to America: A History of Immigration and Ethnicity in American Life; Prisoners Without Trial: Japanese Americans in World War II; *and* Guarding the Golden Door: American Immigration Policy and Immigrants since 1882.

A

Bibliography and Web Sites

The Trial of John Peter Zenger

Books:

Bezanson, Randall P. *How Free Can the Press Be?* Champaign, IL: University of Illinois Press, 2003.

Cook, Timothy E., ed. *Freeing the Presses: The First Amendment in Action.* Baton Rouge, LA: Louisiana State University Press, 2005.

Martin, Richard W. T. *The Free and Open Press: The Founding of American Democratic Press Liberty.* New York: New York University Press, 2001.

Web sites:

First Amendment Center: Press
http://www.firstamendmentcenter.org/Press/index.aspx

World Press Freedom Committee
http://www.wpfc.org/

The Constitutional Convention of 1787

Books:

Collier, Christopher. Decision in Philadelphia: *The Constitutional Convention of 1787*. New York: Random House, 1987.

Labunski, Richard. *James Madison and the Struggle for the Bill of Rights*. New York: Oxford University Press, 2006.

Rakove, Jack N. *Original Meanings: Politics and Ideas in the Making of the Constitution*. New York: A.A. Knopf, 1996.

Web sites:

Exploring Constitutional Law
The Constitutional Convention of 1787
http://www.law.umkc.edu/faculty/projects/ftrials/conlaw/convention1787.html

National Constitution Center
http://www.constitutioncenter.org/

George Washington

Books:

Beeman, Richard R. "The Founding Fathers and Executive Power," *Chronicle of Higher Education*, vol. 52, no. 28 (March 17, 2006): page B12.

Beschloss, Michael R. *Presidential Courage: Brave Leaders and How They Changed America 1789-1989*. New York: Simon & Schuster, 2007.

Kinkopf, Neil. "Inherent Presidential Power and the Constitutional Structure," *Presidential Studies Quarterly*, vol. 37, no. 1 (March 2007): pp. 37-48.

Web sites:

National Endowment for the Humanities
Heroes of History Lecture

http://www.neh.gov/wtp/heroes/reminilecture.html

U.S. Dept. of State
Democracy Papers: The Power of the Presidency
http://usinfo.state.gov/products/pubs/democracy/dmpaper
7.htm

Victory of the Common School Movement
Books:
Cremin, Lawrence A. *American Education: The Colonial Experience, 1607-1783.* New York: Harper & Row, 1970.

Eakin, Sybil. "Giants of American Education: Horace Mann," *TQ: TECHNOS Quarterly for Education and Technology*, vol. 9, no. 2 (Summer 2000): p4.
(http://www.ait.net/technos/tq _09/2eakin.php)

Reese, William J. *America's Public Schools: From The Common School to "No Child Left Behind."* Baltimore, MD: Johns Hopkins University Press, 2005.

Web sites:
Center for Public Education
http://www.centerforpubliceducation.org

Center on Education Policy
http://www.cep-dc.org

The Sherman Anti-Trust Act of 1890
Books:
High, Jack C., and Wayne E. Gable. *A Century of The Sherman Act: American Economic Opinion, 1890-1990.* Fairfax, VA: George Mason University Press, 1992.

Hovenkamp, Herbert. *The Antitrust Enterprise: Principle and Execution.* Cambridge, MA: Harvard University Press, 2005.

Letwin, William. *Law and Economic Policy in America: The Evolution of the Sherman Antitrust Act.* Chicago: University of Chicago Press, 1981.

Web sites:
Cornell Law School: Antitrust
http://www.law.cornell.edu/wex/index.php/Antitrust

Department of Justice: Antitrust Division
http://www.usdoj.gov/atr/

The Interstate Highway System

Books:
Altshuler, Alan, and David Luberoff. *Mega-Projects: The Changing Politics of Urban Public Investment.* Washington, DC: Brookings Institution Press and Lincoln Institute of Land Policy, 2003.

Davies, Pete. *American Road: The Story of an Epic Transcontinental Journey at the Dawn of the Motor Age.* New York: Henry Holt and Company, 2002.

McNichol, Dan. *The Roads That Built America.* New York: Sterling Publishing Co., Inc., 2005.

Web sites:
American Association of State Highway and Transportation Officials The Interstate Is 50
http://www.interstate50th.org/

U.S. Dept. of Transportation
Dwight D. Eisenhower National System of Interstate and Defense Highways
http://www.fhwa.dot.gov/programadmin/interstate.cfm

The GI Bill of Rights

Books:

Bibliography and Web Sites

Bennett, Michael J. *When Dreams Came True: The GI Bill and the Making of Modern America*. London: Brassey's, 1996.

Humes, Edward. *Over Here: How the G.I. Bill Transformed the American Dream*. New York: Harcourt, 2006.

Mettler, Suzanne. *Soldiers to Citizens: The G.I. Bill and the Making of the Greatest Generation*. New York: Oxford University Press, 2005.

Web sites:
Franklin D. Roosevelt Presidential Library and Museum
Our Documents: The G.I. Bill
http://www.fdrlibrary.marist.edu/odgibill.html

Dept. of Veterans Affairs
G.I. Bill Web site
http://www.gibill.va.gov

The Marshall Plan

Books:
Agnew, John, and J. Nicholas Entrikin, eds. *The Marshall Plan Today: Model and Metaphor*. New York: Routledge, 2004.

Machado, Barry. *In Search of a Usable Past: The Marshall Plan and Postwar Reconstruction Today*. Lexington, VA: George C. Marshall Foundation, 2007.

Schain, Martin A., ed. *The Marshall Plan: Fifty Years After*. New York: Palgrave Macmillan, 2001.

Web sites:
George C. Marshall Foundation
http://www.marshallfoundation.org/

Truman Presidential Library and Museum
Establishing the Marshall Plan

http://www.trumanlibrary.org/whistlestop/study_collection
s/marshall/large/

Brown v. Board of Education

Books:

Greenberg, Jack. *Crusaders in the Court: Legal Battles of the Civil Rights Movement.* Anniversary Edition. New York: Twelve Tables Press, 2004.

Klarman, Michael J. *From Jim Crow to Civil Rights: The Supreme Court and the Struggle for Racial Equality.* New York: Oxford University Press, 2003.

Kluger, Richard. *Simple Justice: The History of Brown v. Board of Education and Black America's Struggle for Equality.* rev. ed. New York: Knopf, 2004.

Web sites:

Smithsonian Institution
National Museum of American History
Separate Is Not Equal: Brown v. Board of Education
http://americanhistory.si.edu/brown/

U.S. Dept. of the Interior
National Park Service
Brown v. Board of Education Historical Site
http://www.nps.gov/brvb/

The Right to Legal Counsel

Books:

Epps, Garrett. *Democracy Reborn: The Fourteenth Amendment and the Fight for Equal Rights in Post-Civil War America.* New York: Henry Holt, 2006.

"Gideon at 40: Facing the Crisis, Fulfilling the Promise," *The American Criminal Law Review*, vol. 41, no. 1 (Winter 2004): p.135.

Bibliography and Web Sites

Lewis, Anthony. *Gideon's Trumpet*. New York: Knopf, 1989.

Web sites:
American Bar Association
Indigent Defense/Public Defender Systems
http://www.abanet.org/legalservices/sclaid/defender/hom
e.html

Landmark Cases: Supreme Court
Gideon v. Wainwright
http://www.landmarkcases.org/gideon/home.html

The Immigration Act of 1965
Books:
Daniels, Roger. *Guarding the Golden Door: American Immigration Policy and Immigrants Since 1882*. New York: Hill and Wang, 2004.

Hing, Bill Ong. *Defining America Through Immigration Policy*. Philadelphia, PA: Temple University Press, 2004.

Zolberg, Aristide R. *A Nation by Design: Immigration Policy in the Fashioning of America*. Cambridge, MA: Harvard University Press, 2006.

Web sites:
Center for Immigration Studies
http://www.cis.org/

Department of Homeland Security: Immigration
http://www.dhs.gov/ximgtn/

www.ingramcontent.com/pod-product-compliance
Lightning Source LLC
Chambersburg PA
CBHW060037040426
42331CB00032B/994